Smythe Gambrell Library

Dedicated to the Glory of God
and
Presented in Loving Memory
of
Mr. and Mrs. Carlyle Fraser
Beloved Benefactors and Friends

Augsburg
Story Bible

Illustrated by Annegert Fuchshuber

Texts from the New Revised Standard Version Bible
condensed by Rolf E. Aaseng

Augsburg
MINNEAPOLIS

AUGSBURG STORY BIBLE

Cover illustration: Annegert Fuchshuber

Library of Congress Cataloging-in-Publication Data

Aaseng, Rolf E.
    Augsburg story Bible / illustrated by Annegert Fuchshuber :
texts from the New Revised Standard Version Bible
condensed by Rolf E. Aaseng.
        p.   cm.
    Includes index.
    Summary: A retelling of many familiar stories from both
the Old and New Testaments.
    ISBN 0-8066-2607-0 (alk. paper)
    1. Bible—Paraphrases, English.   2. Bible stories, English.
[1. Bible stories.   2. Bible—Selections.]   I. Fuchshuber,
Annegert, ill.   II. Augsburg Publishing House.   III. Title.
IV. Title: Story Bible.
BS551.2.A27   1992
220.9'505—dc20   92-2527
                                                            CIP
                                                             AC

The paper used in this publication meets the minimum requirements of American National Standard for Information Sciences—Permanence of Paper for Printed Library Materials, ANSI Z329.48-1984. ∞™

Manufactured in Germany   AF 9-2607
    96   95   94   93   92   1   2   3   4   5   6   7   8   9   10

Contents

A Word to Young Readers

This book introduces Bible stories for today by combining striking and detailed illustrations with the actual words of the Bible. The artist's illustrations help us understand how different the biblical world is from what we are familiar with, and help us use our imaginations to try and enter that world. For example, the characters are not shown as typical North Americans or Europeans, but more as people might have looked in the ancient Near East.

But even as the pictures tell us about the culture and customs of another time, they also remind us that God continues to speak to our lives and to our world today. The illustrations for Jesus' Sermon on the Mount include reminders of how much meaning his words have had for the twentieth century—from the Holocaust to Mother Teresa. And one of the pictures of Job in his suffering (p. 176) is based on a World War II photograph of a man in the Jewish ghetto in Warsaw, Poland, before the ghetto was destroyed by the Nazis.

The 142 stories in this book use the actual words of the Bible, from the New Revised Standard Version, shortened to fit the available space. In a few places, words have been added to make transitions read more smoothly, and these words and phrases are printed in *italic* type.

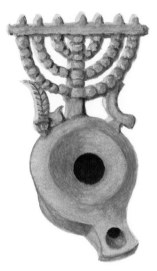

Old
Testament
Stories

The Beginning

God Creates the World

In the beginning when God created the heavens and the earth, the earth was a formless void and darkness covered the face of the deep, while a wind from God swept over the face of the waters.

Then God said, "Let there be light"; and there was light. And God saw that the light was good. God called the light Day, and the darkness Night. And there was evening and morning, the first day.

And God said, "Let there be a dome in the midst of the waters." So God made the dome. God called the dome Sky. And there was evening and morning, the second day.

And God said, "Let the waters under the sky be gathered together into one place, and let the dry land appear." And it was so. God called the dry land Earth, and the waters he called Seas. And God saw that it was good. Then God said, "Let the earth put forth vegetation: plants yielding seed, and fruit trees of every kind." And it was so. And God saw that it was good. And there was evening and there was morning, the third day.

And God said, "Let there be lights in the dome of the sky to give light upon the earth." And it was so. God made two great lights—the greater light to rule the day and the lesser light to rule the night—and the stars. And God saw that it was good. And there was evening and morning, the fourth day.

And God said, "Let the waters bring forth living creatures, and let birds fly above the earth." So God created the great sea monsters and every living creature with which the waters swarm, and every winged bird. And God saw that it was good. God blessed them, saying, "Be fruitful and multiply and fill the waters in the seas, and let birds multiply on the earth." And there was evening and morning, the fifth day.

And God said, "Let the earth bring forth living creatures." And it was so. God made the wild animals and the cattle and everything that creeps upon the ground. And God saw that it was good.

Then God said, "Let us make humankind in our image, and let them have dominion over the fish and the birds and the cattle and all the wild animals."

So God created humankind in his image, male and female he created them.

God blessed them, and God said to them, "Be fruitful and multiply, and fill the earth and subdue it." And God saw everything that he had made, and indeed, it was very good. And there was evening and morning, the sixth day.

On the seventh day God finished the work that he had done, and he rested. So God blessed the seventh day and hallowed it, because on it God rested.

Ejected from Eden

In the day that the LORD God made the earth and the heavens, the LORD God formed man from the dust of the ground. And the LORD God planted a garden in Eden, and there he put the man whom he had formed.

And the LORD God commanded the man, "You may freely eat of every tree of the garden; but of the tree of the knowledge of good and evil you shall not eat."

Then the LORD God said, "It is not good that the man should be alone; I will make him a helper as his partner." So the LORD God caused a deep sleep to fall upon the man; then he took one of his ribs. And the rib he made into a woman and brought her to the man.

Now the serpent was more crafty than any other wild animal.

He said to the woman, "Did God say, 'You shall not eat from any tree in the garden'?" The woman said, "We may eat of the fruit of the trees in the garden; but God said, 'You shall not eat of the fruit of the tree that is in the middle of the garden, or you shall die.'" But the serpent said, "You will not die; when you eat of it you will be like God, knowing good and evil." So when the woman saw that the tree was good for food, she took of its fruit and ate; and she also gave some to her husband.

Then they heard the sound of the LORD God walking in the garden and the man and his wife hid themselves. But the LORD God called to the man, "Where are you?" He said, "I heard the sound of you in the garden, and I was afraid."

He said, "Have you eaten from the tree of which I commanded you not to eat?" The man said, "The woman whom you gave to be with me gave me fruit from the tree, and I ate." Then the LORD God said to the woman, "What is this that you have done?" The woman said, "The serpent tricked me, and I ate." The LORD God said to the serpent,

"Because you have done this,
    cursed are you among all animals;
upon your belly you shall go,
    and dust you shall eat
    all the days of your life.
I will put enmity between you and the woman,
    and between your offspring and hers;
he will strike your head,
    and you will strike his heel."

To the woman he said, "In pain you shall bring forth children."

And to the man he said,

"Cursed is the ground because of you.
    By the sweat of your face
        you shall eat bread
    until you return to the ground,
        for out of it you were taken."

The man named his wife Eve, because she was the mother of all living. And the LORD God made garments of skins for the man and for his wife, and clothed them.

Then the LORD God sent him forth from the garden of Eden, to till the ground from which he was taken. At the east of the garden of Eden he placed the cherubim, and a sword to guard the way to the tree of life.

Cain and Abel

Now the *man's wife Eve gave birth to* Cain. Next she bore his brother Abel. Now Abel was a keeper of sheep, and Cain a tiller of the ground. In the course of time Cain brought to the LORD an offering of the fruit of the ground, and Abel brought of the firstlings of his flock, their fat portions. And the LORD had regard for Abel and his offering, but for Cain and his offering he had no regard. So Cain was very angry. The LORD said to Cain, "Why are you angry? If you do well, will you not be accepted? And if you do not do well, sin is lurking at the door, but you must master it."

Cain said to his brother Abel, "Let us go out to the field." And when they were in the field, Cain rose up against his brother Abel, and killed him.

Then the LORD said to Cain, "Where is your brother Abel?" He said, "I do not know; am I my brother's keeper?" And the LORD said, "What have you done? Listen; your brother's blood is crying

out to me from the ground! And now you are cursed from the ground, which has opened its mouth to receive your brother's blood from your hand. When you till the ground, it will no longer yield to you its strength; you will be a fugitive and a wanderer on the earth."

Cain said to the LORD, "My punishment is greater than I can bear! Today you have driven me away from the soil, and I shall be hidden from your face; I shall be a fugitive and a wanderer on the earth, and anyone who meets me may kill me." Then the LORD said to him, "Not so! Whoever kills Cain will suffer a sevenfold vengeance." And the LORD put a mark on Cain, so that no one who came upon him would kill him.

Adam's wife bore another son and named him Seth, for she said, "God has appointed for me another child instead of Abel, because Cain killed him."

Noah's Ark

When people began to multiply on the *earth, they became* corrupt in God's sight. And God said to Noah, "I have determined to make an end of all flesh, for the earth is filled with violence because of them. Make yourself an ark of cypress wood. I am going to bring a flood of waters on the earth. Everything that is on the earth shall die. But I will establish my covenant with you; and you shall come into the ark, you, your sons, your wife, and your sons' wives with you. And of every living thing, you shall bring two of every kind into the ark, to keep them alive with you. Also take with you every kind of food that is eaten, and store it up; and it shall serve as food for you and for them."

Noah did all that the LORD had commanded him.

After seven days rain fell on the earth forty days and forty nights. The waters increased greatly and the ark floated. All the high mountains were covered. And all flesh died, all creatures and all human beings. Only Noah was left, and those that were with him in the ark. And the waters swelled on the earth for one hundred fifty days.

But God remembered Noah and all the animals that were with him in the ark. And God made a wind blow over the earth, and the waters gradually receded. The ark came to rest on the mountains of Ararat.

At the end of forty days Noah opened the window of the ark and sent out the raven; and it went to and fro until the waters were dried up from the earth. Then he sent out the dove to see if the waters had subsided. But the dove found no place to set its foot, and it returned to him. He waited another seven days, and again he sent out the dove. The dove came back to him in the evening, and in its beak was a freshly plucked olive leaf; so Noah knew that the waters had subsided. Then he waited another seven days, and sent out the dove; and it did not return.

Then God said to Noah, "Go out of the ark. Bring out with you every living thing that is with you." So Noah went out with his sons and his wife and his sons' wives. And every animal and every bird went out of the ark by families.

Then Noah built an altar to the Lord, and offered burnt offerings on the altar. And the Lord said in his heart, "I will never again destroy every living creature as I have done.

> As long as the earth endures,
> seedtime and harvest, cold and heat,
> summer and winter, day and night,
> shall not cease."

God said to Noah and his sons, "I am establishing my covenant with you and your descendants: never again shall there be a flood to destroy the earth. I have set my bow in the clouds, and it shall be a sign of the covenant between me and the earth. When the bow is in the clouds, I will see it and remember the everlasting covenant between God and every living creature."

The Tower of Babel

Now the whole earth had one language and the same words. And as *people became more numerous and* migrated from the east, they came upon a plain in the land of Shinar and settled there.

And they said to one another, "Come, let us make bricks, and burn them thoroughly." And they had brick for stone, and bitumen for mortar. Then they said, "Come, let us build ourselves a city, and a tower with its top in the heavens, and let us make a name for ourselves; otherwise we shall be scattered abroad upon the face of the whole earth."

The LORD came down to see the city and the tower, which mortals had built. And the LORD said, "Look, they are one people, and they have all one language; and this is only the beginning of what they will do; nothing that they propose to do will now be impossible for them. Come, let us go down, and confuse their language, so that they will not understand one another's speech." So the LORD scattered them abroad from there over the face of all the earth, and they left off building the city. Therefore it was called Babel, because there the LORD confused the language of all the earth; and from there the LORD scattered them abroad over the face of all the earth.

Abraham and Sarah

God's Promise to Abram

Now the Lord said to Abram, "Go from your country and your kindred to the land that I will show you. I will make of you a great nation, and I will bless you, and make your name great, and in you all the families of the earth shall be blessed."

So Abram went, as the Lord had told him. Abram took his wife Sarai and his brother's son Lot, and all the possessions that they had gathered, and they set forth. When they had come to the land of Canaan, the Lord appeared to Abram, and said, "To your offspring I will give this land." So he built there an altar to the Lord.

The Lord said to Abram, "Raise your eyes now, and look from the place where you are, northward and southward and eastward and westward; for all the land that you see I will give to you and to your offspring forever. I will make your offspring like the dust of the earth; so that if one can count the dust of the earth, your offspring also can be counted. Rise up, walk through the length and the breadth of the land, for I will give it to you." So Abram moved his tent, and came and settled by the oaks of Mamre, which are at Hebron; and there he built an altar to the Lord.

After these things Abram said, "O Lord God, what will you give me, for I continue childless, and the heir of my house is Eliezer of Damascus?" But the word of the Lord came to him, "This man shall not be your heir; no one but your very own issue shall be your heir." He brought him outside and said, "Look toward heaven and count the stars, if you are able to count them." Then he said to him, "So shall your descendants be." And he believed the Lord; and the Lord reckoned it to him as righteousness.

Then the Lord said to Abram, "Know this for certain, that your offspring shall be aliens in a land that is not theirs, and shall be slaves there, and they shall be oppressed for four hundred years; but I will bring judgment on the nation that they serve, and afterward they shall come out with great possessions.

On that day the LORD made a covenant with Abram, saying, "To your descendants I give this land."

Lot Chooses Sodom

Now Abram was very rich in livestock, in silver, and in gold. Lot, who went with Abram, also had flocks and herds and tents, so that the land could not support both of them living together. And there was strife between the herders of Abram's livestock and the herders of Lot's livestock.

Then Abram said to Lot, "Let there be no strife between you and me, and between your herders and my herders; for we are kindred. Is not the whole land before you? Separate yourself from me. If you take the left hand, then I will go to the right; or if you take the right hand, then I will go to the left." Lot looked about him, and saw that the plain of the Jordan was well watered everywhere like the garden of the LORD, like the land of Egypt. So Lot chose for himself all the plain of the Jordan, and Lot journeyed eastward; thus they separated from each other. Abram settled in the land of Canaan, while Lot settled among the cities of the Plain and moved his tent as far as Sodom. Now the people of Sodom were wicked, great sinners against the LORD.

God Promises a Son

When Abram was ninety-nine years old, the LORD appeared to Abram, and said to him, "I am God Almighty; walk before me, and be blameless. And I will make my covenant between me and you, and will make you exceedingly numerous. No longer shall your name be Abram, but your name shall be Abraham; for I have made you the ancestor of a multitude of nations.

"As for Sarai your wife, you shall not call her Sarai, but Sarah shall be her name. I will bless her, and moreover I will give you a son by her. Kings of people shall come from her." Then Abraham fell on his face and laughed, and said to himself, "Can a child be born to a man who is a hundred years old? Can Sarah, who is ninety years old, bear a child?"

The LORD appeared *again* to Abraham as he sat at the entrance of his tent in the heat of the day. He looked up and saw three men standing near him. When he saw them, he ran to meet them, and bowed down to the ground. He said, "My lord, if I find favor with you, do not pass by your servant. Let a little water be brought, and wash your feet, and rest yourselves under the tree. Let me bring a little bread, that you may refresh yourselves, and after that you may pass on."

So they said, "Do as you have said."

Abraham hastened into the tent to Sarah, and said, "Make ready quickly three measures of choice flour, knead it, and make cakes." Abraham ran to the herd, and took a calf, tender and good, and gave it to the servant, who hastened to prepare it.

Then he took curds and milk and the calf that he had prepared, and set it before them; and he stood by them under the tree while they ate.

They said to him, "Where is your wife Sarah?" And he said, "There, in the tent." Then one said, "I will return to you in due season, and your wife Sarah shall have a son." And Sarah was listening at the tent entrance behind him. Now Abraham and Sarah were old, advanced in age. So Sarah laughed to herself, saying, "After I have grown old, and my husband is old, shall I have pleasure?"

The LORD said to Abraham, "Why did Sarah laugh, and say, 'Shall I indeed bear a child, now that I am old?' Is anything too wonderful for the LORD? At the set time I will return to you, in due season, and Sarah shall have a son."

But Sarah denied, saying, "I did not laugh"; for she was afraid.

Abraham Bargains with God

Then the men set out from there, and they looked toward Sodom; and Abraham went with them to set them on their way.

The LORD said, "Shall I hide from Abraham what I am about to do, seeing that Abraham shall become a great and mighty nation, and all the nations of the earth shall be blessed in him? No, for I have chosen him, that he may charge his children and his household after him to keep the way of the LORD by doing righteousness and justice; so that the LORD may bring about what he has promised him."

Then the LORD said, "How great is the outcry against Sodom and Gomorrah and how very grave their sin! I must go down and see whether they have done altogether according to the outcry that has come to me."

Then Abraham came near and said, "Will you indeed sweep away the righteous with the wicked? Suppose there are fifty righteous within the city; will you then sweep away the place and not forgive it for the fifty righteous who are in it? Far be it from you to do such a thing, to slay the righteous with the wicked. Shall not the Judge of all the earth do what is just?"

And the LORD said, "If I find at Sodom fifty righteous in the city, I will forgive the whole place for their sake."

Abraham answered, "Let me take it upon myself to speak to the LORD, I who am but dust and ashes. Suppose five of the fifty righteous are lacking? Will you destroy the whole city for lack of five?" And he said, "I will not destroy it if I find forty-five there."

Again he spoke to him, "Suppose forty are found there." He answered, "For the sake of forty I will not do it."

Then he said, "Oh do not let the LORD be angry if I speak. Suppose thirty are found there." He answered, "I will not do it, if I find thirty there."

He said, "Let me take it upon myself to speak to the LORD. Suppose twenty are found there." He answered, "For the sake of twenty I will not destroy it."

Then he said, "Oh do not let the LORD be angry if I speak just once more. Suppose ten are found there." He answered, "For the sake of ten I will not destroy it." And the LORD went his way, when he had finished speaking to Abraham, and Abraham returned to his place.

Sodom and Gomorrah Destroyed

Two angels came to Sodom in the evening, and Lot was sitting in the gateway. When Lot saw them, he rose to meet them, and bowed down with his face to the ground. He said, "Please, my lords, turn aside to your servant's house and spend the night, and wash your feet; then you can rise early and go on your way." They said, "No; we will spend the night in the square." But he urged them strongly; so they turned aside to him and entered his house; and he made them a feast, and baked unleavened bread, and they ate.

But before they lay down, the men of the city, the men of Sodom, both young and old, all the people to the last man, surrounded the house; and they called to Lot, "Where are the men who came to you tonight? Bring them out to us." Lot went out of the door to the men, shut the door after him, and said, "I beg you, my brothers, do not act so wickedly. Do nothing to these men, for they have come under the shelter of my roof."

But they replied, "Stand back!" And they said, "This fellow came here as an alien, and he would play the judge! Now we will deal worse with you than with them." Then they pressed hard against the man Lot, and came near the door to break it down. But the men inside reached out their hands and brought Lot into the house with them, and shut the door. And they struck with blindness the men who were at the door of the house, both small and great, so that they were unable to find the door.

Then the men said to Lot, "Have you anyone else here? Sons-in-law, sons, daughters, or anyone you have in the city—bring them out of the place. For we are about to destroy this place, because the outcry against its people has become great before the LORD, and the LORD has sent us to destroy it." So Lot went out and said to his sons-in-law, who were to marry his daughters, "Up, get out of this place; for the LORD is about to destroy the city." But he seemed to his sons-in-law to be jesting.

When morning dawned, the angels urged Lot, saying, "Get up, take your wife and your two daughters who are here, or else you will be consumed in the punishment of the city." But he lingered; so the men seized him and his wife and his two daughters by the hand, the LORD being merciful to him, and they brought him out and left him outside the city.

When they had brought them outside, they said, "Flee for your life; do not look back or stop anywhere in the Plain; flee to the hills, or else you will be consumed." And Lot said to them, "Oh, no, my lords; your servant has found favor with you, and you have shown me great kindness in saving my life; but I cannot flee to the hills, for fear the disaster will overtake me and I die. Look, that city is near enough to flee to, and it is a little one. Let me escape there—is it not a little one?—and my life will be saved!"

He said to him, "Very well, I grant you this favor too, and will not overthrow the city of which you have spoken. Hurry, escape there, for I can do nothing until you arrive there." Therefore the city was called Zoar.

Then the LORD rained on Sodom and Gomorrah sulfur and fire from heaven; and he overthrew those cities, and all the Plain, and all the inhabitants of the cities, and what grew on the ground. But Lot's wife, behind him, looked back, and she became a pillar of salt.

Abraham looked down toward Sodom and Gomorrah and saw the smoke of the land going up like the smoke of a furnace.

So it was that, when God destroyed the cities of the Plain, God remembered Abraham, and set Lot out of the midst of the overthrow, when he overthrew the cities in which Lot had settled.

Isaac Is Born

The LORD did for Sarah as he had promised. Sarah bore Abraham a son in his old age, at the time of which God had spoken. Abraham gave the name Isaac to his son and circumcised Isaac when he was eight days old, as God had commanded him. Abraham was a hundred years old when his son Isaac was born to

him. Now Sarah said, "God has brought laughter for me; everyone who hears will laugh with me. Who would ever have said to Abraham that Sarah would nurse children? Yet I have borne him a son in his old age."

The child grew, and was weaned; and Abraham made a great feast on the day that Isaac was weaned.

Sarah lived one hundred twenty-seven years, and died. Abraham went in to mourn for Sarah and said to the Hittites, "I am a stranger and an alien residing among you; give me property among you for a burying place, so that I may bury my dead out of my sight." The Hittites answered Abraham, "Hear us, my lord; you are a mighty prince among us. Bury your dead in the choicest of our burial places." Abraham weighed out for Ephron four hundred shekels of silver so the field of Ephron passed from the Hittites into Abraham's possession as a burying place.

Rebekah

Now Abraham was old. Abraham said to his servant, "Swear by the LORD, the God of heaven and earth, that you will not get a wife for my son from the daughters of the Canaanites, among whom I live, but will go to my country and to my kindred and get a wife for my son Isaac." The servant said to him, "Perhaps the woman may not be willing to follow me to this land; must I then take your son back to the land from which you came?" Abraham said to him, "If the woman is not willing to follow you, then you will be free from this oath; only you must not take my son back there."

Then the servant took ten camels and departed, and went to the city of Nahor. It was toward evening, the time when women go out to draw water. And he said, "O LORD, God of my master Abraham, please grant me success today. The daughters of the townspeople are coming out to draw water. Let the girl to whom I shall say, 'Please offer your jar that I may drink,' and who shall say, 'Drink, and I will water your camels'—let her be the one whom you have appointed for your servant Isaac. By this I shall know that you have shown steadfast love to my master."

Before he had finished speaking, Rebekah was coming with her water jar on her shoulder. The servant ran to meet her and said, "Please let me sip a little water from your jar." "Drink, my lord," she said, and quickly gave him a drink. When she had finished, she said, "I will draw for your camels also."

When the camels had finished drinking, the man took two bracelets for her arms and said, "Tell me whose daughter you are. Is there room in your father's house for us to spend the night?" She said to him, "I am the daughter of Bethuel. We have plenty of straw and fodder and a place to spend the night." The man bowed his head and worshiped the LORD and said, "Blessed be the LORD, the God of my master Abraham, who has not forsaken my master. The LORD has led me to the house of my master's kin."

Then the girl ran and told her mother about these things. Rebekah had a brother whose name was Laban; and Laban ran

25

to the spring. He said, "Come in, O blessed of the LORD. Why do you stand outside when I have prepared the house and a place for the camels?" So the man came into the house; and Laban unloaded the camels, and gave him straw and fodder for the camels, and water to wash his feet and the feet of the men who were with him. Then food was set before him to eat; but he said,

"I will not eat until I have told my errand." He said, "Speak on."

So he said, "I am Abraham's servant. The LORD has greatly blessed my master, and he has become wealthy. Sarah my master's wife bore a son to my master when she was old. My master made me swear, saying, 'You shall not take a wife for my son from the daughters of the Canaanites, but you shall go to my kindred, and get a wife for my son.'

"I came today to the spring, and said, 'O LORD, the God of my master Abraham, if now you will only make successful the way I am going! I am standing here by the spring of water; let the young woman who comes out to draw, to whom I shall say, "Please give me a little water from your jar to drink," and who will say to me, "Drink, and I will draw for your camels also"— let her be the woman whom the LORD has appointed for my master's son.'

"Before I had finished speaking in my heart, there was Rebekah with her water jar on her shoulder. I said to her, 'Please let me drink.' She quickly let down her jar and said, 'Drink, and I will also water your camels.' Then I asked her, 'Whose daughter are you?' She said, 'The daughter of Bethuel.' Then I bowed my head and worshiped the LORD, and blessed the LORD, the God of my master Abraham, who had led me to the daughter of my master's kinsman for his son."

Then Laban and Bethuel answered, "The thing comes from the LORD. Look, Rebekah is before you; take her and go, and let her be the wife of your master's son, as the LORD has spoken."

When Abraham's servant heard their words, he bowed himself to the ground before the LORD. And the servant brought out jewelry of silver and of gold, and garments, and gave them to Rebekah; he also gave to her brother and to her mother costly ornaments. Then he and the men who were with him ate and drank, and they spent the night there.

When they rose in the morning, he said, "Send me back to my master." Her brother and her mother said, "Let the girl remain with us a while, at least ten days; after that she may go." But he said to them, "Do not delay me, since the LORD has made my journey successful; let me go to my master." They said, "We will call the girl, and ask her."

And they called Rebekah, and said to her, "Will you go with this man?" She said, "I will." So they sent away their sister Rebekah and her nurse along with Abraham's servant and his men. And they blessed Rebekah and said to her,

> "May you, our sister, become
>   thousands of myriads;
> may your offspring gain possession
>   of the gates of their foes."

Then Rebekah and her maids mounted the camels, and followed the man.

Now Isaac went out in the evening to walk in the field; and looking up, he saw camels coming. And Rebekah looked up, and when she saw Isaac, she said to the servant, "Who is the man walking in the field to meet us?" The servant said, "It is my master." So she took her veil and covered herself. And the servant told Isaac all the things that he had done. Then Isaac took Rebekah, and she became his wife; and he loved her. So Isaac was comforted after his mother's death.

Jacob

The Twins

Isaac was forty years old when he married Rebekah. Isaac prayed to the LORD for his wife, because she was barren; and the LORD granted his prayer, and his wife Rebekah conceived. The children struggled together within her; and she said, "If it is to be this way, why do I live?" And the LORD said to her,

> "Two nations are in your womb,
>   and two peoples born of you shall be divided;
> the one shall be stronger than the other,
>   the elder shall serve the younger."

When her time to give birth was at hand, there were twins. The first came out red, all his body like a hairy mantle; so they named him Esau. Afterward his brother came out, with his hand gripping Esau's heel; so he was named Jacob.

When the boys grew up, Esau was a skillful hunter, a man of the field, while Jacob was a quiet man, living in tents. Isaac loved Esau, because he was fond of game; but Rebekah loved Jacob.

Once when Jacob was cooking a stew, Esau came in from the field, and he was famished. Esau said to Jacob, "Let me eat some of that red stuff, for I am famished!" Jacob said, "First sell me your birthright." Esau said, "I am about to die; of what use is a birthright to me?" Jacob said, "Swear to me first." So he swore to him, and sold his birthright to Jacob. Then Jacob gave Esau bread and lentil stew, and he ate and drank, and rose and went his way. Thus Esau despised his birthright.

Jacob Deceives Isaac

When Isaac was old and his eyes were dim so that he could not see, he called Esau and said to him, "See, I am old; I do not know the day of my death. Take your weapons, your quiver and your bow, and go out to the field, and hunt game for me. Then prepare for me savory food, such as I like, and bring it to me to eat, so that I may bless you before I die."

Now Rebekah was listening. So when Esau went to the field to hunt, Rebekah said to Jacob, "I heard your father say to your brother Esau, 'Bring me game, and prepare for me savory food to eat, that I may bless you before I die.' Now therefore, my son, obey my word. Go to the flock, and get me two choice kids, so that I may prepare from them savory food; and you shall take it to your father to eat, so that he may bless you before he dies."

But Jacob said to his mother, "Look, Esau is a hairy man, and I am a man of smooth skin. Perhaps my father will feel me, and I shall seem to be mocking him, and bring a curse on myself and not a blessing."

His mother said to him, "Let your curse be on me, my son; only obey my word, and go, get them for me." So he went and got them and brought them to his mother; and his mother prepared savory food. Then Rebekah took the best garments of Esau, and put them on Jacob; and she put the skins of the kids on his hands and his neck. Then she handed the savory food, and the bread that she had prepared, to Jacob.

So he went in to his father, and said, "My father"; and he said, "Here I am; who are you, my son?" Jacob said to his father, "I am Esau. I have done as you told me; now sit up and eat of my game, so that you may bless me." But Isaac said to his son, "How is it that you have found it so quickly, my son?" He answered, "Because the LORD your God granted me success."

Then Isaac said to Jacob, "Come near, that I may feel you, to know whether you are really my son Esau or not." So Jacob went up to his father Isaac, who felt him and said, "The voice is Jacob's voice, but the hands are the hands of Esau." He said, "Are you really my son Esau?" He answered, "I am." Then he said, "Bring it to me, that I may eat and bless you." So he brought it to him, and he ate. Then Isaac said, "Come near and kiss me, my son." So he came and kissed him; and he smelled his garments, and blessed him, and said,

"Ah, the smell of my son
      is like the smell of a field that the LORD has blessed.
May God give you of the dew of heaven,
      and of the fatness of the earth,
      and plenty of grain and wine.

Let peoples serve you,
 and nations bow down to you.
Be lord over your brothers,
 and may your mother's sons bow down to you.
Cursed be everyone who curses you,
 and blessed be everyone who blesses you!"

As soon as Isaac had finished blessing Jacob, when Jacob had scarcely gone out from the presence of his father, Esau came in from his hunting. He also prepared savory food, and brought it to his father. And he said, "Let my father sit up and eat of his son's game, so that you may bless me." His father Isaac said to him, "Who are you?" He answered, "I am your firstborn son, Esau." Then Isaac trembled violently, and said, "Who was it then that hunted game and brought it to me, and I ate it all before you came, and I have blessed him?—yes, and blessed he shall be!"

When Esau heard his father's words, he cried out with an exceedingly great and bitter cry, and said, "Bless me also, father!" But he said, "Your brother came deceitfully, and he has taken away your blessing." Esau said, "Is he not rightly named Jacob? For he has supplanted me these two times. He took away my birthright; and now he has taken away my blessing."

Then he said, "Have you not reserved a blessing for me?" Isaac answered Esau, "I have already made him your lord, and I have given him all his brothers as servants, and with grain and wine I have sustained him. What then can I do for you, my son?"

Esau said to his father, "Have you only one blessing, father? Bless me, me also, father!" And Esau lifted up his voice and wept. Then his father Isaac answered him:

"See, away from the fatness of the earth
 shall your home be,
 and away from the dew of heaven on high.
By your sword you shall live,
 and you shall serve your brother;
but when you break loose,
 you shall break his yoke from your neck."

Jacob's Dream

Now Esau hated Jacob and said to himself, "The days of mourning for my father are approaching; then I will kill my brother." But the words of Esau were told to Rebekah; so she called Jacob and said to him, "Your brother Esau is planning to kill you. Flee at once to my brother Laban, and stay with him until your brother forgets what you have done to him."

Then Rebekah said to Isaac, "If Jacob marries one of the women of the land, what good will my life be to me?"

Then Isaac called Jacob and charged him, "You shall not marry one of the Canaanite women. Go at once to your mother's father; and take as wife one of the daughters of Laban, your mother's brother. May God Almighty bless you and make you fruitful and numerous. May he give to you the blessing of Abraham, so that you may take possession of the land where you now live as an alien—land that God gave to Abraham." Thus Isaac sent Jacob away.

Jacob came to a certain place and stayed there for the night, because the sun had set. Taking one of the stones of the place, he put it under his head and lay down. He dreamed that there was a ladder set up on the earth, the top of it reaching to heaven; and the angels of God were ascending and descending on it. And the LORD stood beside him and said, "I am the LORD, the God

of Abraham your father and the God of Isaac; the land on which you lie I will give to you and to your offspring; and your offspring shall be like the dust of the earth, and you shall spread abroad to the west and to the east and to the north and to the south; and all the families of the earth shall be blessed in you and in your offspring. Know that I am with you and will keep you wherever you go, and will bring you back to this land."

Then Jacob woke from his sleep and said, "Surely the LORD is in this place—and I did not know it!" And he was afraid, and said, "How awesome is this place! This is none other than the house of God, and this is the gate of heaven."

So Jacob rose early in the morning, and he took the stone that he had put under his head and set it up for a pillar and poured oil on the top of it. He called that place Bethel. Then Jacob made a vow, saying, "If God will be with me, and will keep me in this way that I go, and will give me bread to eat and clothing to wear, so that I come again to my father's house in peace, then the LORD shall be my God, and this stone, which I have set up for a pillar, shall be God's house; and of all that you give me I will surely give one tenth to you."

Jacob Is Married

Then Jacob went on his journey, and came to a well and three flocks of sheep lying there beside it. Jacob said to *the shepherds,* "Where do you come from?" They said, "We are from Haran." He said to them, "Do you know Laban?" They said, "We do, and here is his daughter Rachel, coming with the sheep."

When Jacob saw Rachel, the daughter of his mother's brother Laban, Jacob went up and rolled the stone from the well's mouth, and watered the flock. And Jacob told Rachel that he was Rebekah's son; and she ran and told her father.

When Laban heard the news about his sister's son Jacob, he ran to meet him, and brought him to his house. And he stayed with him a month.

Then Laban said to Jacob, "Because you are my kinsman, should you serve me for nothing? Tell me, what shall your wages be?" Now Laban had two daughters: Leah and Rachel. Jacob loved Rachel; so he said, "I will serve you seven years for Rachel." Laban said, "It is better that I give her to you than that I should give her to any other man; stay with me." So Jacob served seven years for Rachel, and they seemed to him but a few days because of the love he had for her.

Then Jacob said to Laban, "Give me my wife, for my time is completed." So Laban gathered together all the people, and made a feast. But in the evening he took his daughter Leah and brought her to Jacob. When morning came, it was Leah! And Jacob said to Laban, "What have you done to me? Did I not serve with you for Rachel? Why then have you deceived me?"

Laban said, "This is not done in our country—giving the younger before the firstborn. We will give you the other also in return for serving me another seven years." Jacob did so, and Laban gave him Rachel as a wife. Jacob loved Rachel more than Leah.

Leah bore a son, and named him Reuben; she said, "Surely now my husband will love me." She again bore a son, and named him Simeon. Again she bore a son; he was named Levi. She again bore a son, and named him Judah.

When Rachel saw that she bore Jacob no children, she envied her sister. So she gave him her maid Bilhah as a wife. And Bilhah bore Jacob a son. Rachel named him Dan. Rachel's maid Bilhah bore Jacob a second son. Rachel named him Naphtali.

When Leah saw that she had ceased bearing children, she took her maid Zilpah and gave her to Jacob as a wife. Then Leah's maid Zilpah bore Jacob a son. And Leah named him Gad. Leah's maid Zilpah bore Jacob a second son. And Leah named him Asher.

Then Leah conceived and bore Jacob a fifth son. Leah named him Issachar. And Leah bore Jacob a sixth son; she named him Zebulun. Afterwards she bore a daughter, and named her Dinah.

Then Rachel bore a son, and said, "God has taken away my reproach"; and she named him Joseph.

When Rachel had borne Joseph, Jacob said to Laban, "Give me my wives and my children and let me go; for you know very well the service I have given you." Laban said to him, "The LORD has blessed me because of you; name your wages, and I will give it."

Jacob said, "You shall not give me anything, if you will do this for me, I will again feed your flock and keep it; let me pass through all your flock today, removing from it every speckled and spotted sheep and every black lamb, and the spotted and speckled among the goats; and such shall be my wages. So my honesty will answer for me later, when you come to look into my wages with you. Every one that is not speckled and spotted among the goats and black among the lambs, if found with me, shall be counted stolen."

Laban said, "Good! Let it be as you have said." But that day Laban removed the male goats that were striped and spotted, and all the female goats that were speckled and spotted, every one that had white on it, and every lamb that was black.

Then Jacob took fresh rods of poplar and almond and plane, and peeled white streaks in them, exposing the white of the rods. He set the rods in front of the flocks in the watering places. And since they bred when they came to drink, the flocks bred in front of the rods, and produced young that were striped, speckled, and spotted.

Jacob separated the lambs, and did not put them with Laban's flock. Thus the man grew exceedingly rich, and had large flocks, and camels and donkeys.

Jacob Leaves Laban

Now Jacob heard that the sons of Laban were saying, "Jacob has taken all that was our father's; he has gained all this wealth from what belonged to our father." And Jacob saw that Laban did not regard him as favorably as he did before. Then the LORD said to Jacob, "Return to the land of your ancestors, and I will be with you."

So Jacob arose, and set his children and his wives on camels; and he drove away all his livestock that he had gained, to go to the land of Canaan.

On the third day Laban was told that Jacob had fled. So he pursued him for seven days until he caught up with him. But God came to Laban in a dream, and said to him, "Take heed that you say not a word to Jacob, either good or bad."

Laban said to Jacob, "Why did you flee secretly and not tell me? I would have sent you away with mirth and songs. And why did you not permit me to kiss my sons and my daughters farewell? What you have done is foolish." Jacob answered Laban, "Because I was afraid, for I thought that you would take your daughters from me by force."

Then Jacob said to Laban, "What is my offense that you have hotly pursued me? These twenty years I have been with you; your ewes and your female goats have not miscarried, and I have not eaten the rams of your flocks. That which was torn by wild beasts I did not bring to you; I bore the loss of it myself. I served you fourteen years for your two daughters, and six years for your flock, and you have changed my wages ten times. If the God of my father, the God of Abraham and the Fear of Isaac, had not been on my side, surely now you would have sent me away empty-handed."

Then Laban said to Jacob, "Come now, let us make a covenant, you and I; and let it be a witness between you and me." So Jacob took a stone, and set it up as a pillar.

Laban said, "The LORD watch between you and me, when we are absent one from the other. If you ill-treat my daughters, or

if you take wives in addition to my daughters though no one else is with us, remember that God is witness between you and me."

"This pillar is a witness, that I will not pass beyond to you, and you will not pass beyond this pillar to me, for harm. May the God of Abraham judge between us."

Early in the morning Laban rose up, and kissed his grandchildren and his daughters and blessed them; then he departed and returned home.

Jacob Wrestles with God

Jacob went on his way and the angels of God met him; and when Jacob saw them he said, "This is God's camp!"

Jacob sent messengers before him to his brother Esau, instructing them, "Thus you shall say to my lord Esau: Thus says your servant Jacob, 'I have lived with Laban as an alien, and stayed until now; and I have oxen, donkeys, flocks, male and female slaves; and I have sent to tell my lord, in order that I may find favor in your sight.'"

The messengers returned to Jacob, saying, "We came to your brother Esau, and he is coming to meet you, and four hundred men are with him." Then Jacob was greatly afraid and distressed; and he divided the people that were with him, and the flocks and herds and camels, into two companies, thinking, "If Esau comes to the one company and destroys it, then the company that is left will escape."

And Jacob said, "O God of my father Abraham and God of my father Isaac, O LORD who said to me, 'Return to your country and to your kindred, and I will do you good,' I am not worthy of the least of all the steadfast love and all the faithfulness that you have shown to your servant, for with only my staff I crossed this Jordan; and now I have become two companies. Deliver me, please, from the hand of my brother, from the hand of Esau, for I am afraid of him; he may come and kill us all, the mothers with the children. Yet you have said, 'I will surely do you good, and make your offspring as the sand of the sea, which cannot be counted because of their number.' "

So he spent that night there, and from what he had with him he took a present for his brother Esau, two hundred female goats and twenty male goats, two hundred ewes and twenty rams, thirty milch camels and their colts, forty cows and ten bulls, twenty female donkeys and ten male donkeys. These he delivered into the hand of his servants, and said to his servants, "Pass on

ahead of me." He instructed the foremost, "When Esau my brother meets you, and asks you, 'To whom do you belong? Where are you going? And whose are these?' then you shall say, 'They belong to your servant Jacob; they are a present sent to my lord Esau; and moreover he is behind us.' " He likewise instructed all who followed, "You shall say the same thing to Esau when you meet him." For he thought, "I may appease him with the present that goes ahead of me, and perhaps he will accept me."

The same night he got up and took his two wives, his two maids, and his eleven children, and crossed the ford of the Jabbok. He took them and sent them across the stream. Jacob was

left alone; and a man wrestled with him until daybreak. When the man saw that he did not prevail against Jacob, he struck him on the hip socket; and Jacob's hip was put out of joint.

Then he said, "Let me go, for the day is breaking." But Jacob said, "I will not let you go, unless you bless me." So he said to him, "What is your name?" And he said, "Jacob."

Then the man said, "You shall no longer be called Jacob, but Israel, for you have striven with God and with humans, and have prevailed." And he blessed him. Jacob called the place Peniel, saying, "For I have seen God face to face, and yet my life is preserved."

The Brothers Make Peace

Now Jacob looked up and saw Esau coming, and four hundred men with him. So he divided the children among Leah and Rachel and the two maids. He put the maids with their children in front, then Leah with her children, and Rachel and Joseph last of all. He himself went on ahead of them, bowing himself to the ground seven times, until he came near his brother.

But Esau ran to meet him, and embraced him, and they wept. When Esau saw the women and children, he said, "Who are these with you?" Jacob said, "The children whom God has graciously given your servant." Then the maids drew near, they and their children, and bowed down; Leah likewise and her children drew near and bowed down; and finally Joseph and Rachel drew near, and they bowed down.

Esau said, "What do you mean by all this company that I met?" Jacob answered, "To find favor with my lord." But Esau said, "I have enough, my brother; keep what you have for yourself." Jacob said, "No, please; if I find favor with you, then accept my present from my hand; for truly to see your face is like seeing the face of God—since you have received me with such favor.

Please accept my gift that is brought to you, because God has dealt graciously with me, and because I have everything I want." So he urged him, and he took it.

Then Esau said, "Let us journey on our way, and I will go alongside you."

But Jacob said to him, "My lord knows that the children are frail and that the flocks and herds, which are nursing, are a care to me; and if they are overdriven for one day, all the flocks will die. Let my lord pass on ahead of his servant, and I will lead on slowly, according to the pace of the cattle that are before me and according to the pace of the children, until I come to my lord in Seir."

So Esau returned that day.

God said to Jacob, "Arise, go up to Bethel, and settle there. Make an altar there to the God who appeared to you when you fled from your brother Esau."

Then they journeyed from Bethel; and Rachel was in childbirth. When she was in her hard labor, the midwife said to her, "Do not be afraid; for now you will have another son." As her soul was departing (for she died), she named him Ben-oni; but his father called him Benjamin.

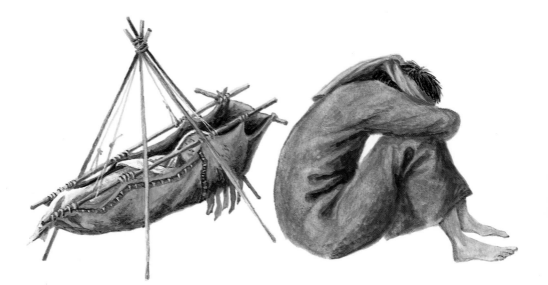

Joseph and His Brothers

Joseph the Dreamer

Jacob settled in the land where his father had lived as an alien, the land of Canaan. This is the story of the family of Jacob.

Joseph, being seventeen years old, was shepherding the flock with his brothers; he was a helper to the sons of Bilhah and Zilpah, his father's wives; and Joseph brought a bad report of them to their father. Now Israel loved Joseph more than any other of his children, because he was the son of his old age; and he had made him a long robe with sleeves. But when his brothers saw that their father loved him more than all his brothers, they hated him.

Once Joseph had a dream, and when he told it to his brothers, they hated him even more. He said to them, "Listen to this dream that I dreamed. There we were, binding sheaves in the field. Suddenly my sheaf rose and stood upright; then your sheaves gathered around it, and bowed down to my sheaf."

His brothers said to him, "Are you indeed to reign over us?" So they hated him even more because of his dreams and his words.

He had another dream, and told it to his brothers, saying, "I have had another dream: the sun, the moon, and eleven stars were bowing down to me."

But when he told it to his father and to his brothers, his father rebuked him, and said to him, "What kind of dream is this? Shall we indeed come, I and your mother and your brothers, and bow to the ground before you?"

So his brothers were jealous of him, but his father kept the matter in mind.

The Brothers Sell Joseph

Now his brothers went to pasture their father's flock near Shechem. And Israel said to Joseph, "Are not your brothers pasturing the flock at Shechem? Come, I will send you to them." He answered, "Here I am."

So he said to him, "Go now, see if it is well with your brothers and with the flock; and bring word back to me." So he sent him from the valley of Hebron.

He came to Shechem, and a man found him wandering in the fields; the man asked him, "What are you seeking?" "I am seeking my brothers," he said; "tell me, please, where they are pasturing the flock." The man said, "They have gone away, for I heard them say, 'Let us go to Dothan.'"

So Joseph went after his brothers, and found them at Dothan. They saw him from a distance, and before he came near to them, they conspired to kill him. They said to one another, "Here comes this dreamer. Come now, let us kill him and throw him into one of the pits; then we shall say that a wild animal has devoured him, and we shall see what will become of his dreams."

But when Reuben heard it, he delivered him out of their hands, saying, "Let us not take his life." Reuben said to them, "Shed no blood; throw him into this pit here in the wilderness, but lay no hand on him"—that he might rescue him out of their hand and restore him to his father. So when Joseph came to his brothers, they stripped him of his robe, the long robe with sleeves that he wore; and they took him and threw him into a pit. The pit was empty; there was no water in it.

Then they sat down to eat; and looking up they saw a caravan of Ishmaelites coming from Gilead, with their camels carrying gum, balm, and resin, on their way to carry it down to Egypt. Then Judah said to his brothers, "What profit is it if we kill our brother and conceal his blood? Come, let us sell him to the Ishmaelites, and not lay our hands on him, for he is our brother, our own flesh." And his brothers agreed.

When some Midianite traders passed by, they drew Joseph up, lifting him out of the pit, and sold him to the Ishmaelites for twenty pieces of silver. And they took Joseph to Egypt.

When Reuben returned to the pit and saw that Joseph was not in the pit, he tore his clothes. He returned to his brothers, and said, "The boy is gone; and I, where can I turn?" Then they

took Joseph's robe, slaughtered a goat, and dipped the robe in the blood. They had the long robe with sleeves taken to their father, and they said, "This we have found; see now whether it is your son's robe or not."

He recognized it, and said, "It is my son's robe! A wild animal has devoured him; Joseph is without doubt torn to pieces."

Then Jacob tore his garments, and put sackcloth on his loins, and mourned for his son many days. All his sons and all his daughters sought to comfort him; but he refused to be comforted, and said, "No, I shall go down to Sheol to my son, mourning." Thus his father bewailed him.

Meanwhile the Midianites had sold him in Egypt to Potiphar, one of Pharaoh's officials, the captain of the guard.

Potiphar Puts Joseph in Prison

The LORD was with Joseph, and he became a successful man in the house of his Egyptian master. His master saw that the LORD was with him, and that the LORD caused all that he did to prosper. So he made him overseer of his house and put him in charge of all that he had. From the time that he made him overseer, the LORD blessed the Egyptian's house for Joseph's sake.

Now Joseph was handsome and good-looking. And after a time his master's wife cast her eyes on Joseph and said, "Lie with me."

But he refused and said to his master's wife, "My master has put everything that he has in my hand. He is not greater in this house than I am, nor has he kept back anything from me except yourself, because you are his wife. How then could I do this great wickedness, and sin against God?" And although she spoke to Joseph day after day, he would not consent to lie beside her or to be with her.

One day, however, when he went into the house to do his work, and while no one else was in the house, she caught hold of his garment, saying, "Lie with me!" But he left his garment in her hand, and ran outside. When she saw that he had left his garment, she called out to the members of her household and said to them, "See, my husband has brought among us a Hebrew to insult us! He came in to lie with me, and I cried out with a loud voice; and when he heard me cry out, he left his garment beside me, and fled outside." Then she kept his garment until his master came home, and she told him the same story, saying, "The Hebrew servant, whom you have brought among us, came in to me to insult me; but as soon as I cried out, he left his garment beside me, and fled outside."

When his master heard the words that his wife spoke to him, he became enraged. And Joseph's master took him and put him into the prison. But the LORD was with Joseph and gave him favor in the sight of the chief jailer. The chief jailer committed to Joseph's care all the prisoners who were in the prison. The chief jailer paid no heed to anything that was in Joseph's care, because the LORD was with him; and whatever he did, the LORD made it prosper.

Joseph Interprets Dreams

Some time after this, the cupbearer of the king of Egypt and his baker offended the king. Pharaoh was angry with his two officers, and he put them in custody in the house of the captain of the guard, in the prison where Joseph was confined. The captain of the guard charged Joseph with them, and he waited on them; and they continued for some time in custody.

One night they both dreamed, each his own dream, and each dream with its own meaning. When Joseph came to them in the morning, he saw that they were troubled. So he asked Pharaoh's officers, who were with him in custody in his master's house, "Why are your faces downcast today?"

They said to him, "We have had dreams, and there is no one to interpret them."

And Joseph said to them, "Do not interpretations belong to God? Please tell them to me."

So the chief cupbearer told his dream to Joseph, and said to him, "In my dream there was a vine before me, and on the vine there were three branches. As soon as it budded, its blossoms came out and the clusters ripened into grapes. Pharaoh's cup was in my hand; and I took the grapes and pressed them into Pharaoh's cup, and placed the cup in Pharaoh's hand."

Then Joseph said to him, "This is its interpretation: the three

branches are three days; within three days Pharaoh will lift up your head and restore you to your office; and you shall place Pharaoh's cup in his hand, just as you used to do when you were his cupbearer. But remember me when it is well with you; please do me the kindness to make mention of me to Pharaoh, and so get me out of this place. For in fact I was stolen out of the land of the Hebrews; and here also I have done nothing that they should have put me into the dungeon."

When the chief baker saw that the interpretation was favorable, he said to Joseph, "I also had a dream: there were three cake baskets on my head, and in the uppermost basket there were all sorts of baked food for Pharaoh, but the birds were eating it out of the basket on my head."

And Joseph answered, "This is its interpretation: the three baskets are three days; within three days Pharaoh will lift up

your head—from you!—and hang you on a pole; and the birds will eat the flesh from you."

On the third day, which was Pharaoh's birthday, he made a feast for all his servants. He restored the chief cupbearer to his cupbearing, and he placed the cup in Pharaoh's hand; but the chief baker he hanged, just as Joseph had interpreted to them. Yet the chief cupbearer did not remember Joseph, but forgot him.

Pharaoh's Dreams

After two years, Pharaoh dreamed that he was standing by the Nile, and there came up out of the Nile seven sleek and fat cows, and they grazed in the reed grass. Then seven other cows, ugly and thin, came up out of the nile after them, and stood by the other cows on the bank of the Nile. The ugly and thin cows ate up the seven sleek and fat cows. And Pharaoh awoke.

Then he fell asleep and dreamed a second time; seven ears of grain, plump and good, were growing on one stalk. Then seven ears, thin and blighted by the east wind, sprouted after them. The thin ears swallowed up the seven plump and full ears. Pharaoh awoke, and it was a dream.

In the morning his spirit was troubled; so he sent and called for all the magicians of Egypt and all its wise men. Pharaoh told them his dreams, but there was no one who could interpret them.

Then the chief cupbearer said to Pharaoh, "Once Pharaoh put me and the chief baker in custody. We dreamed, he and I. A young Hebrew was there with us, a servant of the captain of the guard. When we told him, he interpreted our dreams to us. As he interpreted to us, so it turned out; I was restored to my office, and the baker was hanged."

Then Pharaoh sent for Joseph, and he was hurriedly brought out of the dungeon. Pharaoh said to Joseph, "I have had a dream, and no one can interpret it. I have heard that when you hear a dream you can interpret it." Joseph answered Pharaoh, "It is not I; God will give Pharaoh a favorable answer."

Then Pharaoh said, "In my dream I was standing on the banks of the Nile; and seven cows, fat and sleek, came up out of the Nile and fed in the reed grass. Then seven other cows came up after them, poor, very ugly, and thin. Never had I seen such ugly ones in all the land of Egypt. The thin and ugly cows ate up the first seven fat cows, but they were still as ugly as before. Then I awoke. I fell asleep a second time and I saw in my dream seven ears of grain, full and good, growing on one stalk, and seven ears, withered, thin, and blighted by the east wind, sprouting after them; and the thin ears swallowed up the seven good ears."

Then Joseph said to Pharaoh, "Pharaoh's dreams are one and the same; God has revealed what he is about to do. The seven good cows are seven years, and the seven good ears are seven years. The seven lean and ugly cows are seven years, as are the seven empty ears blighted by the east wind. There will come seven years of great plenty throughout all the land of Egypt. After them there will arise seven years of famine, and all the plenty will be forgotten. The doubling of Pharaoh's dream means that the thing is fixed by God, and God will shortly bring it about.

"Now therefore let Pharaoh select a man who is discerning and wise, and set him over the land of Egypt. Let Pharaoh appoint overseers, and take one-fifth of the produce of the land during the seven plenteous years. Let them gather all the food of these good years and keep it. That food shall be a reserve against the seven years of famine."

The proposal pleased Pharaoh. Pharaoh said to his servants, "Can we find anyone else like this—one in whom is the spirit of God?"

So Pharaoh said to Joseph, "Since God has shown you all this, there is no one so discerning and wise as you. You shall be over my house, and all my people shall order themselves as you command; only with regard to the throne will I be greater than you."

Removing his signet ring from his hand, Pharaoh put it on Joseph's hand; he arrayed him in garments of fine linen, and put a gold chain around his neck. He had him ride in the chariot of his second-in-command; and they cried out in front of him, "Bow the knee!" Thus he set him over all the land of Egypt.

During the seven plenteous years, he gathered up all the food and stored it.

Joseph's Brothers Go to Egypt

The seven years of plenty in the land of Egypt came to an end; and the seven years of famine began, just as Joseph had said. There was famine in every country, but throughout the land of Egypt there was bread. When all the land of Egypt was famished, the people cried to Pharaoh for bread. Pharaoh said to the Egyptians, "Go to Joseph; what he says to you, do." And since the famine had spread over all the land, Joseph opened all the storehouses, and sold to the Egyptians for the famine was severe in the land of Egypt. Moreover, all the world came to Joseph in Egypt to buy grain, because the famine became severe throughout the world.

When Jacob learned that there was grain in Egypt, he said to his sons, "Why do you keep looking at one another? I have heard," he said, "that there is grain in Egypt; go down and buy grain for us there, that we may live and not die." So ten of Joseph's brothers went down to buy grain in Egypt. But Jacob did not send Joseph's brother Benjamin with his brothers, for he feared that harm might come to him. Thus the sons of Israel were among the other people who came to buy grain, for the famine had reached the land of Canaan.

Now Joseph was governor over the land; it was he who sold to all the people of the land. And Joseph's brothers came and bowed themselves before him with their faces to the ground. When Joseph saw his brothers, he recognized them, but he treated them like strangers and spoke harshly to them. "Where do you come from?" he said. They said, "From the land of Canaan, to buy food." Although Joseph had recognized his brothers, they did not recognize him. Joseph also remembered the dreams that he had dreamed about them.

He said to them, "You are spies; you have come to see the nakedness of the land!"

They said to him, "No, my lord; your servants have come to buy food. We are honest men; your servants have never been spies. We, your servants, are twelve brothers, the sons of a certain man in the land of Canaan; the youngest, however, is now with our father, and one is no more."

But Joseph said to them, "It is just as I have said to you; you are spies! Here is how you shall be tested: as Pharaoh lives, you shall not leave this place unless your youngest brother comes here! Let one of you go and bring your brother, while the rest of you remain in prison, in order that your words may be tested, whether there is truth in you." And he put them all together in prison for three days.

On the third day Joseph said to them, "Do this and you will live, for I fear God: if you are honest men, let one of your brothers stay here where you are imprisoned. The rest of you shall go and carry grain for the famine of your households, and bring your youngest brother to me. Thus your words will be verified, and you shall not die." And they agreed to do so.

They said to one another, "Alas, we are paying the penalty for what we did to our brother; we saw his anguish when he pleaded with us, but we would not listen. That is why this anguish has come upon us."

Then Reuben answered them, "Did I not tell you not to wrong the boy? But you would not listen. So now there comes a reckoning for his blood." They did not know that Joseph understood them, since he spoke with them through an interpreter. He turned away from them and wept. And he picked out Simeon and had him bound before their eyes. Joseph then gave orders to fill their bags with grain, to return every man's money to his sack, and to give them provisions for their journey. This was done for them.

They loaded their donkeys with their grain, and departed.

Hungry Again

When one of them opened his sack to give his donkey fodder at the lodging place, he saw his money at the top of the sack. He said to his brothers, "My money has been put back; here it is in my sack!" At this they turned trembling to one another, saying, "What is this that God has done to us?"

When they came to their father Jacob, they told him all that had happened, saying, "The man, the lord of the land, spoke harshly to us, and charged us with spying. But we said to him, 'We are honest men. We are twelve brothers; one is no more, and the youngest is now with our father in the land of Canaan.' Then the man said to us, 'By this I shall know that you are honest men: leave one of your brothers with me, take grain for the famine of your households, and go your way. Bring your youngest brother to me, and I shall know that you are not spies but honest men. Then I will release your brother to you, and you may trade in the land.' "

Their father Jacob said to them, "I am the one you have bereaved of children: Joseph is no more, and Simeon is no more, and now you would take Benjamin."

Then Reuben said to his father, "You may kill my two sons if I do not bring him back to you. Put him in my hands, and I will bring him back to you." But he said, "My son shall not go down

with you, for his brother is dead, and he alone is left. If harm should come to him, you would bring down my gray hairs with sorrow to Sheol."

Now the famine was severe in the land. And when they had eaten up the grain that they had brought from Egypt, their father said to them, "Go again, buy us a little more food." But Judah said, "The man solemnly warned us, saying, 'You shall not see my face unless your brother is with you.'"

Israel said, "Why did you tell the man that you had another brother?" They replied, "The man questioned us about ourselves, saying, 'Is your father still alive? Have you another brother?' What we told him was in answer to these questions. Could we in any way know that he would say, 'Bring your brother down'?" Then Judah said to his father Israel, "Send the boy with me; you can hold me accountable for him. If I do not bring him back to you, then let me bear the blame forever."

Then Israel said to them, "If it must be so, then do this: take some of the choice fruits of the land in your bags, and carry them down as a present to the man—a little balm, honey, pistachio nuts, and almonds. Carry back with you the money that was returned in the top of your sacks; perhaps it was an oversight. Take your brother also, and may God Almighty grant you mercy before the man, so that he may send back your other brother and Benjamin. As for me, if I am bereaved of my children, I am bereaved." So the men went on their way down to Egypt.

The Second Trip to Egypt

When Joseph saw Benjamin with them, he said to the steward of his house, "Bring the men into the house, and slaughter an animal and make ready, for the men are to dine with me at noon." The man did as Joseph said.

Now the men were afraid because they were brought to Joseph's house, and they said, "It is because of the money replaced in our sacks, that we have been brought in, so that he may have an opportunity to fall upon us, to make slaves of us and take our donkeys." So they went to the steward and spoke with him. They said, "Oh, my lord, we came down the first time to buy food; and when we came to the lodging place we opened our sacks, and there was each one's money in the top of his sack. So we have brought it back with us. Moreover we have brought down with us additional money to buy food. We do not know who put our money in our sacks."

He replied, "Do not be afraid; your God and the God of your father must have put treasure in your sacks for you; I received your money." Then he brought Simeon out to them.

When the steward had brought the men into Joseph's house, and given them water, and they had washed their feet, and when he had given their donkeys fodder, they made the present ready for Joseph's coming at noon, for they had heard that they would dine there.

When Joseph came home, they brought him the present that they had carried into the house, and bowed to the ground before him. He inquired about their welfare, and said, "Is your father well, the old man of whom you spoke? Is he still alive?" They said, "Your servant our father is well." And they bowed their heads and did obeisance. Then he looked up and saw his brother Benjamin, his mother's son, and said, "Is this your youngest brother, of whom you spoke to me? God be gracious to you, my son!" With that, Joseph hurried out, because he was overcome with affection for his brother, and he was about to weep. So he went into a private room and wept there.

Then he washed his face and came out; and controlling himself he said, "Serve the meal." They served him by himself, and them by themselves, and the Egyptians who ate with him by themselves, because the Egyptians could not eat with the Hebrews, for that is an abomination to the Egyptians. When they were seated before him, the firstborn according to his birthright and the youngest according to his youth, the men looked at one another in amazement. Portions were taken to them from Joseph's table, but Benjamin's portion was five times as much as any of theirs. So they drank and were merry with him.

Then he commanded the steward, "Fill the men's sacks with

food, as much as they can carry, and put each man's money in the top of his sack. Put my cup, the silver cup, in the top of the sack of the youngest, with his money for the grain." And he did as Joseph told him.

Reunion

As soon as the morning was light, the men were sent away with their donkeys. When they had gone only a short distance from the city, Joseph said to his steward, "Go, follow after the men; and when you overtake them, say to them, 'Why have you returned evil for good? Why have you stolen my silver cup? Is it not from this that my lord drinks? Does he not indeed use it for divination? You have done wrong in doing this.'"

When he overtook them, he repeated these words to them. They said to him, "Why does my lord speak such words as these? Far be it from your servants that they should do such a thing! Look, the money that we found at the top of our sacks, we brought back to you from the land of Canaan; why then would we steal silver or gold from your lord's house? Should it be found with any one of your servants, let him die; moreover the rest of us will become my lord's slaves."

He said, "Even so; in accordance with your words, let it be: he with whom it is found shall become my slave, but the rest of you shall go free."

Then each one quickly lowered his sack to the ground, and each opened his sack. He searched, beginning with the eldest and ending with the youngest; and the cup was found in Benjamin's sack. At this they tore their clothes. Then each one loaded his donkey, and they returned to the city.

Judah and his brothers came to Joseph's house while he was still there; and they fell to the ground before him. Joseph said to them, "What deed is this that you have done? Do you not know that one such as I can practice divination?"

And Judah said, "What can we say to my lord? What can we speak? How can we clear ourselves? God has found out the guilt of your servants; here we are then, my lord's slaves, both we and also the one in whose possession the cup has been found."

But he said, "Far be it from me that I should do so! Only the one in whose possession the cup was found shall be my slave; but as for you, go up in peace to your father."

Then Judah stepped up to him and said, "O my lord, let your servant please speak a word in my lord's ears, and do not be angry with your servant; for you are like Pharaoh himself. When I come to my father and the boy is not with us, then, as his life is bound up in the boy's life, when he sees that the boy is not with us, he will die; and your servants will bring down the gray hairs of your servant our father with sorrow to Sheol. Please let your servant remain as a slave to my lord in place of the boy;

and let the boy go back with his brothers. For how can I go back to my father if the boy is not with me? I fear to see the suffering that would come upon my father."

Then Joseph could no longer control himself and he cried out, "Send everyone away from me." So no one stayed with him when Joseph made himself known to his brothers. And he wept so loudly that the Egyptians heard it. Joseph said to his brothers, "I am Joseph. Is my father still alive?" But his brothers could not answer him, so dismayed were they at his presence.

Then Joseph said to his brothers, "Come closer to me." And they came closer. He said, "I am your brother, Joseph, whom you sold into Egypt. And now do not be distressed, or angry with yourselves, because you sold me here; for God sent me before you to preserve life. God has made me a father to Pharoah, and lord of all his house and ruler over all the land of Egypt. Hurry and go up to my father and say to him, 'Thus says your son Joseph, God has made me lord of all Egypt; come down to me, do not delay.'" Then he kissed all his brothers, and wept upon them, and after that his brothers talked with him.

Joseph gave them wagons according to the instruction of Pharaoh, and he gave them provisions for the journey. So they went up out of Egypt and came to their father Jacob. And they told him, "Joseph is still alive! He is even ruler over all the land of Egypt." He was stunned and could not believe them. But when they told him all the words of Joseph, and when he saw the wagons that Joseph had sent to carry him, the spirit of their father Jacob revived. Israel said, "Enough! My son Joseph is still alive. I must go and see him before I die."

Then Jacob set out; and the sons of Israel, their little ones, and their wives, in the wagons that Pharaoh had sent to carry him. They also took their livestock and the goods that they had acquired in the land of Canaan, and they came into Egypt.

Then Joseph brought in his father Jacob, and presented him before Pharaoh, and Jacob blessed Pharaoh.

Thus Israel settled in the land of Egypt, in the region of Goshen; and they gained possessions in it, and were fruitful and multiplied exceedingly.

Moses

Moses Is Saved by Pharaoh's Daughter

Joseph lived one hundred ten years. Then Joseph said to his brothers, "I am about to die; but God will surely come to you, and bring you up out of this land to the land that he swore to Abraham, to Isaac, and to Jacob."

Then Joseph died, and all his brothers, and that whole generation. But the Israelites were fruitful and prolific; they multiplied and grew exceedingly strong, so that the land was filled with them.

Now a new king arose over Egypt, who did not know Joseph. He said to his people, "Look, the Israelite people are more numerous and more powerful than we. Come, let us deal shrewdly with them, or they will increase and, in the event of war, join our enemies and fight against us and escape from the land."

Therefore they set taskmasters over them to oppress them with forced labor. They built supply cities, Pithom and Rameses, for Pharaoh. But the more they were oppressed, the more they multiplied and spread, so that the Egyptians came to dread the Israelites. The Egyptians became ruthless in imposing tasks on the Israelites, and made their lives bitter with hard service in mortar and brick and in every kind of field labor.

The king of Egypt said to the Hebrew midwives, one of whom was named Shiphrah and the other Puah, "When you act as midwives to the Hebrew women, if it is a boy, kill him; but if it is a girl, she shall live." But the midwives feared God; they did not do as the king of Egypt commanded them, but they let the boys live.

So the king of Egypt summoned the midwives and said to them, "Why have you done this, and allowed the boys to live?"

The midwives said to Pharaoh, "Because the Hebrew women are not like the Egyptian women; for they are vigorous and give birth before the midwife comes to them." So God dealt well with the midwives; and the people multiplied and became very strong. And because the midwives feared God, he gave them families.

Then Pharaoh commanded all his people, "Every boy that is born to the Hebrews you shall throw into the Nile, but you shall let every girl live."

Now a man from the house of Levi went and married a Levite woman. The woman bore a son; and when she saw that he was a fine baby, she hid him three months. When she could hide him no longer she got a papyrus basket for him, and plastered it with bitumen and pitch; she put the child in it and placed it among the reeds on the bank of the river. His sister stood at a distance, to see what would happen to him.

The daughter of Pharaoh came down to bathe at the river, while her attendants walked beside the river. She saw the basket among the reeds and sent her maid to bring it. When she opened it, she saw the child. He was crying, and she took pity on him, "This must be one of the Hebrews' children," she said.

Then his sister said to Pharaoh's daughter, "Shall I go and get you a nurse from the Hebrew women to nurse the child for you?" Pharaoh's daughter said to her, "Yes."

So the girl went and called the child's mother. Pharaoh's daughter said to her, "Take this child and nurse it for me, and I will give you your wages." So the woman took the child and nursed it. When the child grew up, she brought him to Pharaoh's daughter, and she took him as her son. She named him Moses, "because," she said, "I drew him out of the water."

Moses Goes into Exile

One day, after Moses had grown up, he went out to his people and saw their forced labor. He saw an Egyptian beating a Hebrew, one of his kinsfolk. He looked this way and that, and seeing no one he killed the Egyptian and hid him in the sand.

When he went out the next day, he saw two Hebrews fighting; and he said to the one who was in the wrong, "Why do you strike your fellow Hebrew?"

He answered, "Who made you a ruler and judge over us? Do you mean to kill me as you killed the Egyptian?"

Then Moses was afraid and thought, "Surely the thing is known." When Pharaoh heard of it, he sought to kill Moses.

But Moses fled from Pharaoh. He settled in the land of Midian, and sat down by a well. The priest of Midian had seven daughters. They came to draw water, and filled the troughs to water their father's flock. But some shepherds came and drove them away. Moses got up and came to their defense and watered their flock.

When they returned to their father, he said, "How is it that you have come back so soon today?"

They said, "An Egyptian helped us against the shepherds; he even drew water for us and watered the flock."

He said to his daughters, "Where is he? Why did you leave the man? Invite him to break bread."

Moses agreed to stay with the man, and he gave Moses his daughter Zipporah in marriage. She bore a son, and he named him Gershom; for he said, "I have been an alien residing in a foreign land."

After a long time the king of Egypt died. The Israelites groaned under their slavery, and cried out. Out of the slavery their cry for help rose up to God. God heard their groaning, and God remembered his covenant with Abraham, Isaac, and Jacob. God looked upon the Israelites, and God took notice of them.

The Burning Bush

Moses was keeping the flock of his father-in-law; he led his flock beyond the wilderness, and came to Horeb, the mountain of God. There the angel of the LORD appeared to him in a flame of fire out of a bush; he looked, and the bush was blazing, yet it was not consumed. Then Moses said, "I must turn aside and look at this great sight, and see why the bush is not burned up."

When the LORD saw that he had turned aside to see, God called to him out of the bush, "Moses, Moses!" And he said, "Here I am." Then he said, "Come no closer! Remove the sandals from your feet, for the place on which you are standing is holy ground." He said further, "I am the God of your father, the God of Abraham, the God of Isaac, and the God of Jacob." And Moses hid his face, for he was afraid to look at God.

Then the LORD said, "I have observed the misery of my people who are in Egypt; I have heard their cry. Indeed, I know their sufferings, and I have come down to deliver them from the Egyptians, and to bring them to a good and broad land, a land flowing with milk and honey. So come, I will send you to Pharaoh to bring my people out of Egypt." But Moses said to God, "Who am I that I should go to Pharaoh, and bring the Israelites out of Egypt?" He said, "I will be with you; and this shall be the sign that it is I who sent you: when you have brought the people out of Egypt, you shall worship God on this mountain."

But Moses said to God, "If I come to the Israelites and say to them, 'The God of your ancestors has sent me to you,' and they ask me, 'What is his name?' what shall I say to them?" God said to Moses, "I AM WHO I AM. You shall say to the Israelites, 'I AM has sent me to you.'

"Go and assemble the elders of Israel, and say to them, 'The LORD, the God of your ancestors, the God of Abraham, of Isaac, and of Jacob, has appeared to me, saying: I have given heed to what has been done to you in Egypt. I will bring you up out of the misery of Egypt, to the land of the Canaanites, a land flowing with milk and honey.' They will listen to your voice; and you and the elders of Israel shall go to the king of Egypt and say to him, 'The LORD, the God of the Hebrews, has met with us; let

יהוה

us now go a three days' journey into the wilderness, so that we may sacrifice to the LORD our God.' I know, however, that the king of Egypt will not let you go unless compelled by a mighty hand. So I will stretch out my hand and strike Egypt with all my wonders; after that he will let you go."

Then Moses answered, "But suppose they do not believe me or listen to me, but say, 'The LORD did not appear to you.'" The LORD said to him, "What is that in your hand?" He said, "A staff." And he said, "Throw it on the ground." So he threw the staff on the ground, and it became a snake; and Moses drew back from it.

Then the LORD said to Moses, "Reach out your hand, and seize it by the tail"—so he reached out his hand and grasped it, and it became a staff in his hand—"so that they may believe that the LORD, the God of their ancestors, the God of Abraham, the God of Isaac, and the God of Jacob, has appeared to you."

Again, the LORD said to him, "Put your hand inside your cloak." He put his hand into his cloak; and when he took it out, his hand was leprous, as white as snow. Then God said, "Put your hand back into your cloak"—so he put his hand back into his cloak, and when he took it out, it was restored like the rest of his body. "If they will not believe you or heed the first sign, they may believe the second sign. If they will not believe even these two signs or heed you, you shall take some water from the Nile and pour it on the dry ground; and the water that you shall take from the Nile will become blood on the dry ground."

But Moses said to the LORD, "O my LORD, I have never been eloquent; I am slow of speech and slow of tongue." Then the LORD said to him, "Who gives speech to mortals? Is it not I, the LORD? Now go, and I will teach you what you are to speak."

But he said, "O my LORD, please send someone else." Then the anger of the LORD was kindled against Moses and he said, "What of your brother Aaron, the Levite? I know that he can speak fluently; even now he is coming out to meet you, and when he sees you his heart will be glad. You shall put the words in his mouth; and he shall speak for you to the people. I will teach you what you shall do."

Moses Goes to Pharaoh

Moses went back to his father-in-law Jethro and said to him, "Please let me go back to my kindred in Egypt and see whether they are still living." And Jethro said to Moses, "Go in peace." So Moses took his wife and his sons, put them on a donkey and went back to the land of Egypt; and Moses carried the staff of God in his hand.

The LORD said to Aaron, "Go into the wilderness to meet Moses." So he met him. Moses told Aaron all the words of the LORD. Then Moses and Aaron assembled the elders of the Israelites. Aaron spoke all the words that the LORD had spoken to Moses. The people believed; and when they heard that the LORD had seen their misery, they bowed down and worshiped.

Afterward Moses and Aaron went to Pharaoh and said, "Thus says the LORD, the God of Israel, 'Let my people go, so that they may celebrate a festival to me in the wilderness.'"

But Pharaoh said, "Who is the LORD, that I should heed him and let Israel go? I do not know the LORD, and I will not let Israel go. Why are you taking the people from their work?"

That same day Pharaoh commanded the taskmasters, "You shall no longer give the people straw to make bricks, as before; let them go and gather straw for themselves. But you shall require of them the same quantity of bricks as they have made previously; for they are lazy; that is why they cry, 'Let us go and offer sacrifice to our God.' "

So the taskmasters said to the people, "Go and get straw yourselves, but your work will not be lessened in the least.' " The supervisors of the Israelites were beaten, and were asked, "Why did you not finish the required quantity of bricks?"

Then the supervisors came to Pharaoh and cried, "Why do you treat your servants like this?"

He said, "You are lazy; that is why you say, 'Let us go and sacrifice to the LORD.' "

As they left Pharaoh, they came upon Moses and Aaron. They said to them, "The LORD look upon you and judge! You have brought us into bad odor with Pharaoh and his officials, and have put a sword in their hand to kill us."

Then Moses turned to the LORD and said, "O LORD, why have you mistreated this people? Why did you ever send me? Since I first came to Pharaoh, he has mistreated this people, and you have done nothing at all to deliver your people."

The Ten Plagues

Then the LORD said to Moses, "Go to Pharaoh. Say to him, 'The LORD, the God of the Hebrews, sent me to you to say, "Let my people go, so that they may worship me in the wilderness." But you have not listened.' Thus says the LORD, "By this you shall know that I am the LORD. I will strike the water that is in the Nile, and it shall be turned to blood."

In the sight of Pharaoh *Aaron* struck the river, and all the water was turned into blood, and the fish died. But the magicians of Egypt did the same by their secret arts; so Pharaoh's heart remained hardened, and he would not listen to them.

Seven days passed. Then the LORD said to Moses, "Go to Pharaoh and say to him, 'Thus says the LORD: Let my people go, so

that they may worship me. If you refuse, I will plague your whole country with frogs. They shall come into your palace, into your bed, and into your ovens and kneading bowls.'" So Aaron stretched out his hand over the waters of Egypt; and the frogs came up and covered the land of Egypt.

Then Pharaoh called Moses and Aaron, and said, "Pray to the LORD to take away the frogs, and I will let the people go to sacrifice to the LORD."

Then Moses cried out to the LORD concerning the frogs and the frogs died. And they gathered them together in heaps, and the land stank. But when Pharaoh saw that there was a respite, he hardened his heart.

Then the LORD said to Moses, "Say to Aaron, 'Stretch out your staff and strike the dust of the earth.'" And Aaron struck the dust

and the dust turned into gnats throughout the whole land of Egypt. The magicians tried to produce gnats by their secret arts, but they could not. The magicians said to Pharaoh, "This is the finger of God!" But Pharaoh would not listen to them.

Then the LORD said to Moses, "Present yourself before Pharaoh, and say to him, 'Thus says the LORD: Let my people go. If you will not, I will send swarms of flies on you.'" The LORD did so, and great swarms of flies came into the house of Pharaoh and into his officials' houses.

Then Pharaoh summoned Moses and Aaron, and said, "Go, sacrifice to your God within the land." But Moses said, "It would not be right to do so; for the sacrifices that we offer are offensive to the Egyptians. We must go into the wilderness and sacrifice to the LORD our God as he commands us." So Pharaoh said, "I will let you go to sacrifice to the LORD your God in the wilderness, provided you do not go very far away."

So Moses prayed to the LORD. And the LORD removed the swarms of flies. But Pharaoh hardened his heart this time also, and would not let the people go.

Then the LORD said to Moses, "Go to Pharaoh, and say to him, 'Thus says the LORD, the God of the Hebrews: Let my people go. If you still hold them, the hand of the LORD will strike with a deadly pestilence your livestock.' " The next day the livestock of the Egyptians died, but of the livestock of the Israelites not one died. But the heart of Pharaoh was hardened.

Then the LORD said to Moses and Aaron, "Take handfuls of soot and throw it in the air." So they took soot, and Moses threw it in the air, and it caused festering boils on humans and animals. The magicians could not stand before Moses because the boils afflicted the magicians. But the LORD hardened the heart of Pharaoh, and he would not listen to them.

Then the LORD said to Moses, "Say to *Pharaoh,* 'Thus says the LORD: By now I could have struck you and your people with pestilence, and you would have been cut off from the earth. But I have let you live to show you my power. Tomorrow I will cause the heaviest hail to fall that has ever fallen in Egypt. Every human or animal that is in the open field will die when the hail

comes down.' " Those officials of Pharaoh who feared the word of the LORD hurried their slaves and livestock off to a secure place.

Then Moses stretched out his staff, and the LORD sent thunder and hail, with fire flashing continually in the midst of it. The hail struck down everything that was in the open field. Only in Goshen, where the Israelites were, there was no hail.

Then Pharaoh summoned Moses and Aaron, and said, "I have sinned! Enough of God's thunder and hail! I will let you go." So Moses stretched out his hands to the LORD; then the thunder and the hail ceased. But when Pharaoh saw that the hail had ceased, he sinned once more and hardened his heart.

So Moses and Aaron went to Pharaoh, and said to him, "Thus says the LORD, 'How long will you refuse to humble yourself before me? Tomorrow I will bring locusts into your country. They shall devour the last remnant left after the hail.' "

Pharaoh's officials said to him, "Let the people go, so that they may worship the LORD their God; do you not yet understand that Egypt is ruined?" So Moses and Aaron were brought back to Pharaoh, and he said, "Go, worship the LORD your God! But which ones are to go?" Moses said, "We will go with our sons and daughters and with our flocks and herds." He said to them, "The LORD indeed will be with you, if ever I let your little ones go with you! Plainly, you have some evil purpose in mind. No, never!" And they were driven out from Pharaoh's presence.

So Moses stretched out his staff and the locusts came. They covered the surface, so that the land was black; and they ate all the plants that the hail had left; nothing green was left. Pharaoh hurriedly summoned Moses and Aaron and said, "I have sinned

against the LORD. Pray that he remove this deadly thing." So the LORD changed the wind into a very strong west wind, which lifted the locusts and drove them into the Red Sea. But Pharaoh would not let the Israelites go.

Then the LORD said to Moses, "Stretch out your hand toward heaven so that there may be darkness over the land." So Moses stretched out his hand, and there was dense darkness for three days. People could not see one another, and could not move from where they were; but all the Israelites had light. Then Pharaoh summoned Moses, and said, "Go, worship the LORD. Only your flocks and your herds shall remain behind." But Moses said, "Our livestock also must go with us, for we must choose some of them for the worship of the LORD our God."

Then Pharaoh said to him, "Get away from me! Take care that you do not see my face again, for on the day you see my face you shall die."

The LORD said to Moses, "I will bring one more plague upon Pharaoh and upon Egypt; afterwards he will let you go. About midnight, every firstborn in the land of Egypt shall die. Then there will be a loud cry throughout the whole land of Egypt. Then the officials shall come down, and bow low, saying, 'Leave us, you and all the people who follow you.'"

The Passover

The LORD said to Moses and Aaron, "Tell the whole congregation of Israel to take a lamb *and* slaughter it. They shall take some of the blood and put it on the doorposts of the houses. They shall eat the lamb that same night; anything that remains until the morning you shall burn. This is how you shall eat it: your loins girded, your sandals on your feet, and your staff in your hand; and you shall eat it hurriedly. It is the passover of the LORD. For I will pass through the land of Egypt that night, and I will strike down every firstborn in the land of Egypt, both human beings and animals; on all the gods of Egypt I will execute judgments: I am the LORD. The blood shall be a sign: when I see

the blood, I will pass over you, and no plague shall destroy you when I strike the land of Egypt.

"You shall observe this rite as a perpetual ordinance. When you come to the land that the LORD will give you, as he has promised, you shall keep this observance. And when your children ask you, 'What do you mean by this observance?' you shall say, 'It is the passover sacrifice to the LORD, for he passed over the houses of the Israelites in Egypt, when he struck down the Egyptians.' "

The Israelites did just as the LORD had commanded Moses and Aaron.

At midnight the LORD struck down all the firstborn in the land of Egypt, from the firstborn of Pharaoh who sat on his throne to the firstborn of the prisoner who was in the dungeon, and all the firstborn of the livestock. Then *Pharaoh* summoned Moses and Aaron in the night, and said, "Rise up, go away from my people, both you and the Israelites! Go, worship the LORD, as you said. Take your flocks and your herds and be gone. And bring a blessing on me too!"

The Egyptians urged the people to hasten their departure from the land, for they said, "We shall all be dead." So the people took their dough before it was leavened, with their kneading bowls wrapped up in their cloaks on their shoulders. It was not leavened, because they were driven out of Egypt and could not wait.

On that very day, all the companies of the LORD went out from the land of Egypt.

Finally Free

When the king of Egypt was told that the people had fled, Pharaoh and his officials said, "What have we done, letting Israel leave our service?" So he had his chariot made ready, and took his army with him; and he pursued the Israelites.

As Pharaoh drew near, the Israelites looked back, and there were the Egyptians advancing on them. In great fear the Israelites cried out to the LORD. They said to Moses, "Was it because

there were no graves in Egypt that you have taken us away? It would have been better for us to serve the Egyptians than to die in the wilderness." But Moses said, "Do not be afraid, stand firm, and see the deliverance that the LORD will accomplish for you."

Then the LORD said to Moses, "Tell the Israelites to go forward. But lift up your staff over the sea and divide it, that the Israelites may go into the sea on dry ground. And the Egyptians shall know that I am the LORD."

The angel of God who was going before the Israelite army moved and went behind them; and the pillar of cloud moved from in front of them and came between the army of Egypt and the army of Israel; one did not come near the other all night.

Then Moses stretched out his hand. The LORD drove the sea back by a strong east wind. The Israelites went into the sea on dry ground, the waters forming a wall for them on their right and on their left. The Egyptians pursued, and went into the sea after them. At the morning watch the LORD threw the Egyptian army into panic. He clogged their chariot wheels so that they turned with difficulty. The Egyptians said, "Let us flee from the Israelites, for the LORD is fighting for them."

Then the LORD said to Moses, "Stretch out your hand over the sea, so that the water may come back upon the Egyptians." So Moses stretched out his hand and the sea returned and covered the entire army of Pharaoh.

Thus the LORD saved Israel that day from the Egyptians. Then Moses and the Israelites sang this song to the LORD: "The LORD is my strength and my might, and he has become my salvation."

Then the prophet Miriam, Aaron's sister, took a tambourine; and all the women went out after her. And Miriam sang to them: "Sing to the LORD, for he has triumphed gloriously; horse and rider he has thrown into the sea."

God Provides Manna

Then Moses ordered Israel to set out from the Red Sea. They went three days in the wilderness and found no water. When they came to Marah, they could not drink the water because it was bitter. The people complained against Moses, saying, "What shall we drink?" He cried out to the LORD; and the LORD showed him a piece of wood; he threw it into the water, and the water became sweet.

Then the Israelites complained, "If only we had died in the land of Egypt, when we sat by the fleshpots and ate our fill of bread; for you have brought us out into this wilderness to kill this whole assembly with hunger."

Then the LORD spoke to Moses, "I have heard the complaining of the Israelites; say to them, 'At twilight you shall eat meat, and in the morning you shall have your fill of bread; then you shall know that I am the LORD your God.'"

In the evening quails came up and covered the camp; and in the morning there was a layer of dew around the camp. When the layer of dew lifted, there on the surface of the wilderness was a fine flaky substance, as fine as frost on the ground. When the Israelites saw it, they said, "What is it?" For they did not know what it was. Moses said, "It is the bread that the LORD has given you to eat. The LORD has commanded: 'Gather as much of it as each of you needs.'" The Israelites did so, some gathering more, some less. Those who gathered much had nothing over, and those who gathered little had no shortage. And Moses said to them, "Let no one leave any of it until morning." But they did not listen to Moses; some left part of it until morning, and it bred worms and became foul. And Moses was angry with them. Morning by morning they gathered it, as much as each needed; but when the sun grew hot, it melted.

On the sixth day they gathered twice as much food. Moses said, "This is what the LORD has commanded: 'Tomorrow is a day of solemn rest, a holy sabbath to the LORD; bake what you want to bake and boil what you want to boil, and all that is left over put aside until morning.' " So they put it aside, as Moses commanded them; and it did not become foul.

On the seventh day some of the people went out to gather, and they found none. The LORD said to Moses, "How long will you refuse to keep my instructions? See! The LORD has given you the

sabbath, therefore on the sixth day he gives you food for two days." So the people rested on the seventh day.

The house of Israel called it manna; it was like coriander seed, white, and the taste of it was like wafers made with honey.

The Israelites camped at Rephdim, but there was no water. The people quarreled with Moses, and said, "Give us water to drink. Why did you bring us out of Egypt, to kill us and our children and livestock with thirst?" So Moses cried out to the LORD, "What shall I do with this people? They are almost ready to stone me."

The LORD said to Moses, "Take in your hand the staff with which you struck the Nile. Strike the rock, and water will come out of it, so that the people may drink." Moses did so, in the sight of the elders of Israel.

The Ten Commandments

The Israelites came to Mount Sinai. Then the LORD called to *Moses* from the mountain, "Tell the Israelites: You have seen what I did to the Egyptians, and how I brought you to myself. If you obey my voice and keep my covenant, you shall be my treasured possession out of all the peoples."

So Moses set before them all the words that the Lord had commanded him. The people answered: "Everything that the Lord has spoken we will do." Then the Lord said, "I am going to come to you in a dense cloud, in order that the people may hear when I speak."

On the morning of the third day there was thunder and lightning, as well as a thick cloud on the mountain, and a blast of a trumpet so loud that all the people who were in the camp trembled. Moses brought the people out of the camp to meet God. They took their stand at the foot of the mountain.

Then God spoke all these words:

I am the Lord your God, who brought you out of the land of Egypt. You shall have no other gods before me.

You shall not make for yourself an idol, whether in the form of anything that is in heaven above, or that is on the earth beneath, or that is in the water under the earth.

You shall not make wrongful use of the name of the Lord your God.

Remember the sabbath day, and keep it holy. Six days you shall labor and do all your work. But the seventh day is a sabbath to the Lord your God; you shall not do any work.

Honor your father and your mother, so that your days may be long in the land that the Lord your God is giving you.

You shall not murder.

You shall not commit adultery.

You shall not steal.

You shall not bear false witness against your neighbor.

You shall not covet your neighbor's house; you shall not covet your neighbor's wife, or male or female slave, or ox, or donkey, or anything that belongs to your neighbor.

When the people witnessed the thunder and lightning, and the mountain smoking, they were afraid and said to Moses, "You speak to us, and we will listen; but do not let God speak to us, or we will die." Moses said, "Do not be afraid; for God has come only to test you and to put the fear of him upon you so that you do not sin." Then the people stood at a distance, while Moses drew near to the thick darkness where God was.

The Golden Calf

The LORD said to Moses, "Come up to me on the mountain, and I will give you tablets of stone, with the law and the commandment, which I have written." So Moses entered the cloud, and went up on the mountain for forty days and forty nights.

When the people saw that Moses delayed to come down, they gathered around Aaron, and said to him, "Come, make gods for us; as for this Moses, we do not know what has become of him." Aaron said to them, "Take off the gold rings that are on your ears and bring them to me." He took the gold, formed it in a mold, and cast an image of a calf; and they said, "These are your gods, O Israel, who brought you up out of the land of Egypt!" When Aaron saw this, he said, "Tomorrow shall be a festival to the Lord." They rose early the next day, and offered sacrifices; and the people sat down to eat and drink, and rose up to revel.

The Lord said to Moses, "Go down at once! Your people have acted perversely; they have cast for themselves an image of a calf, and have worshiped it."

Then Moses turned and went down from the mountain, carrying the two tablets of the covenant. As soon as he saw the calf and the dancing, Moses' anger burned hot, and he threw the tablets from his hands and broke them. He took the calf that they had made, burned it with fire, ground it to powder, scattered it on the water, and made the Israelites drink it.

Moses said to Aaron, "What did this people do to you that you have brought so great a sin upon them?" And Aaron said, "You know the people, that they are bent on evil. They said to me, 'Make us gods, who shall go before us.' So I said to them, 'Whoever has gold, take it off '; so they gave it to me, and I threw it into the fire, and out came this calf!"

Moses said to the people, "You have sinned a great sin. But now I will go up to the LORD; perhaps I can make atonement for your sin." So Moses returned to the LORD and said, "Alas, this people has sinned a great sin. But now, if you will only forgive their sin—but if not, blot me out of the book that you have written."

But the LORD said to Moses, "Whoever has sinned against me I will blot out of my book. But now go, lead the people to the place about which I have spoken to you."

The Ark of the Covenant

The Lord said to Moses: "Tell the Israelites to take an offering. And have them make me a sanctuary, so that I may dwell among them. In accordance with all that I show you so you shall make it.

"They shall make an ark of acacia wood; overlay it with pure gold. Make poles of acacia wood by which to carry the ark. You shall put into the ark the covenant that I shall give you.

"Then you shall make a mercy seat of pure gold. Make one cherub at the one end, and one cherub at the other; they shall face one to another. Put the mercy seat on the top of the ark. There I will meet with you, and deliver to you all my commands.

"You shall make a lampstand of pure gold; and there shall be six branches going out of its sides. You shall make a curtain of blue and bring the ark of the covenant within the curtain. The

curtain shall separate the holy place from the most holy. Outside the curtain, set the table and the lampstand. You shall make the altar of acacia wood. Make poles for the altar to be put through the rings when it is carried."

Moses came down from Mount Sinai. As he came down with the two tablets of the covenant in his hand, Moses did not know

that the skin of his face shone because he had been talking with God.

Moses said to all the congregation of the Israelites: This is the thing that the LORD has commanded: Take from among you an offering to the LORD: gold, silver, and bronze; blue, purple, and crimson yarns, and fine linen; goats' hair, tanned rams' skins, and fine leather; acacia wood, oil for the light, spices for the anointing oil and for the fragrant incense, and onyx stones and gems. All who are skillful among you shall come and make *the tabernacle* that the LORD has commanded.

Then the Israelites came, everyone whose spirit was willing, and brought the Lord's offering to be used for the tent of meeting.

In this way all the work of the tabernacle of the tent of meeting was finished. Then they brought the tabernacle to Moses. When Moses saw that they had done all the work just as the LORD had commanded, he blessed them. Then the cloud covered the tent of meeting and the glory of the LORD filled the tabernacle.

War with the Amalekites

Then Amalek came and fought with Israel. Moses said to Joshua, "Choose some men for us and go out, fight with Amalek. Tomorrow I will stand on the top of the hill with the staff of God in my hand." So Joshua did as Moses told him, and fought with Amalek, while Moses, Aaron, and Hur went up to the top of the hill.

Whenever Moses held up his hand, Israel prevailed; and whenever he lowered his hand, Amalek prevailed. But Moses' hands grew weary; so they took a stone and put it under him, and he sat on it. Aaron and Hur held up his hands, one on one side, and the other on the other side; so his hands were steady until the sun set. And Joshua defeated Amalek and his people with the sword.

Then the LORD said to Moses, "Write this as a reminder in a book and recite it in the hearing of Joshua: I will utterly blot out the remembrance of Amalek from under heaven." And Moses built an altar and called it, The LORD is my banner. He said, "A hand upon the banner of the LORD! The LORD will have war with Amalek from generation to generation."

The Report of the Spies

The LORD said to Moses, "Send men to spy out the land of Canaan, which I am giving to the Israelites."

So Moses sent them to spy out the land, and said to them, "Go and see whether the people are strong or weak, whether they are few or many, whether the towns are unwalled or fortified, whether the land is rich or poor. And bring some of the fruit of the land."

So they went up and spied out the land. And they cut down a branch with a single cluster of grapes, and they carried it on a pole between two of them. They also brought some pomegranates and figs.

At the end of forty days they returned. They came to Moses and Aaron and to all the Israelites. And they told him, "The land to which you sent us flows with milk and honey, and this is its fruit. Yet the people who live in the land are strong, and the towns are fortified and very large."

But Caleb said, "Let us go up at once and occupy it, for we are well able to overcome it." Then the men who had gone up with him said, "We are not able to go up against this people, for they are stronger than we. All the people that we saw are of great size. We seemed like grasshoppers to them."

Then all the congregation raised a loud cry, and the people wept. And all the Israelites said, "Would that we had died in Egypt! Or would that we had died in this wilderness! Why is the LORD bringing us into this land to fall by the sword? Would it

not be better for us to go back to Egypt?" So they said to one another, "Let us choose a captain, and go back to Egypt."

Then Joshua and Caleb, who were among those who had spied out the land, tore their clothes and said, "The land is an exceedingly good land. If the LORD is pleased with us, he will give it to us. Do not rebel against the LORD; do not fear the people of the land, for the LORD is with us." But the whole congregation threatened to stone them.

Then the glory of the LORD appeared at the tent of meeting. And the LORD said to Moses, "How long will this people refuse to believe in me, in spite of all the signs that I have done among them? I will strike them with pestilence and disinherit them, and I will make of you a nation greater and mightier than they."

But Moses said to the LORD, "If you kill this people, then the nations who have heard about you will say, 'It is because the LORD was not able to bring this people into the land he swore to give them that he has slaughtered them in the wilderness.' Now, therefore, let the power of the LORD be great in the way that you promised when you spoke, saying,

'The LORD is slow to anger,
and abounding in steadfast love,
forgiving iniquity and transgression.'

Forgive the iniquity of this people according to the greatness of your steadfast love, just as you have pardoned this people, from Egypt even until now."

Then the LORD said, "I do forgive, just as you have asked; nevertheless, none of the people who have seen my glory and the signs that I did in Egypt and in the wilderness, and yet have not obeyed my voice, shall see the land that I swore to give to their ancestors. But my servant Caleb, because he has followed me wholeheartedly, I will bring into the land. Now, turn tomorrow and set out for the wilderness by the way to the Red Sea."

When Moses told these words to the Israelites, the people mourned greatly. They rose early in the morning, saying, "Here we are. We will go up to the place that the LORD has promised, for we have sinned."

But Moses said, "Why do you continue to transgress the command of the LORD? Do not go up. For the Amalekites and the Canaanites will confront you there, and you shall fall by the sword. Because you have turned back from following the LORD, the LORD will not be with you."

But they presumed to go up to the hill country, even though the ark of the covenant of the LORD, and Moses, had not left the camp. Then the Amalekites and the Canaanites who lived in that hill country came down and defeated them.

Joshua Becomes the Leader

Then Moses went up to the top of Pisgah, and the LORD showed him the whole land. The LORD said to him, "This is the land of which I swore to Abraham, to Isaac, and to Jacob, saying, 'I will give it to your descendants'; I have let you see it with your eyes, but you shall not cross over there."

Moses said: "I am now one hundred twenty years old. I am no longer able to get about, and the LORD has told me, 'You shall not cross over this Jordan.' The LORD your God himself will cross over before you. He will destroy these nations before you, and you shall dispossess them."

Then Moses summoned Joshua and said to him, "You are the one who will go with this people into the land that the LORD

has sworn to their ancestors to give them; and you will put them in possession of it. The LORD will not fail you or forsake you."

Then Moses died. He was buried in a valley in the land of Moab, but no one knows his burial place to this day.

Never since has there arisen a prophet in Israel like Moses, whom the LORD knew face to face.

After the death of Moses, the LORD spoke to Joshua, saying, "Now proceed to cross the Jordan, you and all this people, into the land that I am giving to them. Be strong and courageous; for you shall put this people in possession of the land that I swore to their ancestors to give them."

Joshua son of Nun was full of the spirit of wisdom, because Moses had laid his hands on him; and the Israelites obeyed him, doing as the LORD had commanded Moses.

In the Land of Canaan

Rahab Helps the Israelites

Then Joshua sent two men as spies, saying, "Go, view the land, especially Jericho." So they went, and entered the house of a prostitute whose name was Rahab. The king of Jericho was told, "Some Israelites have come here to search out the land." Then the king of Jericho sent orders to Rahab, "Bring out the men who have come to you." But the woman took the two men and hid them. Then she said, "True, the men came to me, but I did not know where they came from. And when it was time to close the gate at dark, the men went out. Where the men went I do not know. Pursue them quickly, for you can overtake them."

Before they went to sleep, she said to the men: "I know that the LORD has given you the land; all the inhabitants of the land melt in fear before you. For we have heard how the LORD dried up the water of the Red Sea before you when you came out of Egypt. The LORD your God is indeed God. Now then, since I have dealt kindly with you, swear to me by the LORD that you in turn will deal kindly with my family." The men said to her, "Our life for yours! If you do not tell this business of ours, then we will deal kindly and faithfully with you when the LORD gives us the land."

Then she let them down by a rope through the window, for her house was on the outer side of the city wall. She said to them, "Go toward the hill country, so that the pursuers may not come upon you." The men said to her, "We will be released from this oath that you have made us swear to you if we invade the land and you do not tie this crimson cord in the window through which you let us down. But if a hand is laid upon any who are with you in the house, we shall bear the responsibility for their death." She said, "According to your words, so be it." She sent them away and they departed. Then she tied the crimson cord in the window.

They departed and went into the hill country and stayed there until the pursuers returned. Then the two men came to Joshua, and told him all that had happened. They said, "Truly the LORD has given all the land into our hands."

The Fall of Jericho

Early in the morning Joshua set out with all the Israelites, and they came to the Jordan. Then Joshua said, "Tomorrow the LORD will do wonders among you." To the priests Joshua said, "Take up the ark of the covenant, and pass on in front of the people."

Joshua then said to the Israelites, "The ark of the covenant of the LORD is going to pass before you into the Jordan. When the soles of the feet of the priests who bear the ark rest in the waters of the Jordan, the waters flowing from above shall be cut off."

So when those who bore the ark had come to the Jordan, the waters flowing from above stood still, rising up in a single heap. Then the people crossed over on dry ground.

Now Jericho was shut up inside and out because of the Israelites. The LORD said to Joshua, "You shall march around the city, all the warriors circling the city once. Thus you shall do for six days, with seven priests bearing trumpets of rams' horns before the ark. On the seventh day you shall march around the city seven times, the priests blowing the trumpets. When they make a long blast all the people shall shout, and the wall of the city will fall down."

So Joshua summoned the priests and said to them, "Take up the ark of the covenant, and have seven priests carry rams' horns in front of the ark." To the people he said, "Go forward and march around the city." So the ark of the LORD went around the city, circling it once; and they spent the night in the camp. They did this for six days.

On the seventh day they marched around the city in the same manner seven times. At the seventh time, when the priests had blown the trumpets, Joshua said to the people, "Shout! For the LORD has given you the city. The city and all that is in it shall be devoted to the LORD for destruction. Only Rahab the prostitute and all who are with her in her house shall live because she hid the messengers we sent." So the people shouted, and the trumpets were blown, and the wall fell down flat; so the people charged straight ahead into the city and captured it.

So Joshua took the whole land, according to all that the LORD had spoken to Moses; and Joshua died at the age of one hundred ten years.

Then the Israelites did evil: they abandoned the LORD who had brought them out of Egypt. They followed other gods, from among the gods of the peoples who were all around them. So the anger of the LORD was kindled against Israel, and he gave them over to plunderers who plundered them, and he sold them into the power of their enemies, so that they could no longer withstand their enemies. And they were in great distress.

Then the LORD raised up judges, who delivered them out of the power of those who plundered them.

Ruth

In the days when the judges ruled, there was a famine in the land, and a certain man of Bethlehem in Judah went to live in the country of Moab. The man was Elimelech and his wife Naomi, and his sons were Mahlon and Chilion. But Elimelech died, and Naomi was left with her two sons. These took Moabite wives; the name of the one was Orpah and the name of the other Ruth. When they had lived there about ten years, both Mahlon and Chilion also died.

Then Naomi started to return to the land of Judah. She said to her two daughters-in-law, "Go back each of you to your mother's house. May the LORD deal kindly with you, as you have dealt with me." Then they wept aloud. Orpah kissed her mother-in-law, but Ruth clung to her.

So she said, "See, your sister-in-law has gone back to her people and to her gods; return after your sister-in-law." But Ruth said,

> "Do not press me to leave you
>   or to turn back from following you!
> Where you go, I will go;

Where you lodge, I will lodge;
  your people shall be my people,
    and your God my God."

So Naomi returned together with Ruth. They came to Beth-lehem at the beginning of the barley harvest.

And Ruth said to Naomi, "Let me go to the field and glean among the ears of grain." She said to her, "Go, my daughter." So she went. As it happened, she came to the part of the field belonging to Boaz, who was of the family of Elimelech. Just then Boaz came from Bethlehem. He said to his servant who was in charge of the reapers, "To whom does this young woman belong?" The servant answered, "She is the Moabite who came back with Naomi. She said, 'Please, let me glean among the sheaves behind the reapers.'"

Then Boaz said to Ruth, "Now listen, my daughter, do not go to glean in another field or leave this one, but keep close to my young women. I have ordered the young men not to bother you. If you get thirsty, go to the vessels and drink from what the young men have drawn."

Then she said to him, "Why have I found favor in your sight, that you should take notice of me, when I am a foreigner?" But Boaz answered her, "All that you have done for your mother-in-law since the death of your husband has been fully told me. May the LORD reward you for your deeds." Then she said, "May I continue to find favor in your sight, my lord, for you have comforted me and spoken kindly to your servant, even though I am not one of your servants."

At mealtime Boaz said to her, "Come here, and eat some of this bread." So she sat beside the reapers, and he heaped up for her some parched grain. When she got up to glean, Boaz instructed his young men, "Let her glean even among the standing sheaves. You must also pull out some handfuls for her from the bundles, and leave them for her to glean."

So she gleaned in the field until evening. Her mother-in-law said to her, "Where did you glean today?" So she said, "The name of the man with whom I worked today is Boaz." Then Naomi said to her daughter-in-law, "Blessed be he by the LORD, whose kindness has not forsaken the living or the dead! The man is a relative of ours, one of our nearest kin. It is better, my daughter, that you go out with his young women, otherwise you might be bothered in another field." So she stayed close to the young women of Boaz, gleaning until the end of the barley and wheat harvests.

Naomi said to her, "My daughter, I need to seek some security for you, so that it may be well with you. Now here is our kinsman Boaz, with whose young women you have been working. See, he is winnowing barley tonight at the threshing floor. Now wash and anoint yourself, and put on your best clothes and go down to the threshing floor; but do not make yourself known to the man until he has finished eating and drinking. When he lies down, observe the place where he lies; then, go and uncover his feet and lie down; and he will tell you what to do."

So she went down to the threshing floor and did just as her mother-in-law had instructed her. When Boaz had eaten and drunk, he went to lie down at the end of the heap of grain. Then she came stealthily and uncovered his feet, and lay down. At midnight the man was startled; there, lying at his feet, was a woman! He said, "Who are you?" She answered, "I am Ruth. Spread your cloak over your servant, for you are next-of-kin."

He said, "May you be blessed by the LORD, my daughter; this last instance of your loyalty is better than the first; you have not gone after young men, whether poor or rich. Do not be afraid,

I will do for you all that you ask, for all the assembly of my people know that you are a worthy woman. But now, though I am a near kinsman, there is another kinsman more closely related than I. If he is not willing to act as next-of-kin for you, then, as the LORD lives, I will act for you."

So she lay at his feet until morning, but got up before one person could recognize another. Then he said, "Bring the cloak

you are wearing and hold it out." So she held it, and he measured out six measures of barley, and put it on her back. She came to her mother-in-law, who said, "How did things go with you, my daughter?" Then she told her all that the man had done for her, saying, "He gave me these six measures of barley, for he said, 'Do not go back to your mother-in-law empty-handed.' " She replied, "Wait, my daughter, for the man will not rest, but will settle the matter today."

No sooner had Boaz gone up to the gate and sat down there than the next-of-kin came passing by. The next-of-kin said, "Take my right of redemption yourself, for I cannot redeem it." So Boaz took Ruth and she became his wife and she bore a son. They named him Obed; he became the father of Jesse, the father of David.

Samuel

There was a man whose name was Elkanah. He had two wives; one was Hannah and the other Peninnah. Peninnah had children, but Hannah had no children. Now this man used to go up year by year from his town to worship the Lord of hosts at Shiloh.

After they had eaten and drunk at Shiloh, Hannah rose and presented herself before the Lord. Now Eli the priest was sitting beside the doorpost of the temple. She was deeply distressed and prayed to the Lord. She made this vow: "O Lord of hosts, if only you will look on the misery of your servant, and will give to your servant a male child, then I will set him before you until the day of his death."

As she continued praying before the Lord, Eli observed her. Hannah was praying silently; only her lips moved, therefore Eli thought she was drunk. So Eli said to her, "How long will you make a drunken spectacle of yourself?" But Hannah answered, "No, my Lord, I have drunk neither wine nor strong drink. But I have been pouring out my soul before the Lord." Then Eli answered, "Go in peace; the God of Israel grant the petition you have made to him."

They went back to their house at Ramah. In due time Hannah conceived and bore a son. She named him Samuel, for she said, "I have asked him of the Lord."

96

When she had weaned him, she brought him to the house of the Lord at Shiloh; and the child was young. And she said, "For this child I prayed. Therefore I have lent him to the Lord; as long as he lives, he is given to the Lord."

She left him there for the Lord.

Hannah prayed and said,
"My heart exults in the Lord;
   my strength is exalted in my God.
My mouth derides my enemies,
   because I rejoice in my victory.
Those who were full have hired
   themselves out for bread,
but those who were hungry are
   fat with spoil.
The barren has borne seven,
   but she who has many children is forlorn."

Now the boy Samuel continued to grow both in stature and in favor with the LORD and with the people. Samuel was ministering to the LORD under Eli. The word of the LORD was rare in those days; visions were not widespread.

At that time Eli, whose eyesight had begun to grow dim so that he could not see, was lying down in his room. Samuel was lying down in the temple of the LORD, where the ark of God was. Then the LORD called, "Samuel! Samuel!" and he said, "Here I am!" and ran to Eli, and said, "Here I am, for you called me."

But he said, "I did not call; lie down again."

So he went and lay down. The LORD called again, "Samuel!" Samuel got up and went to Eli, and said, "Here I am, for you called me."

But he said, "I did not call, my son; lie down again."

The LORD called Samuel, a third time. And he got up and went to Eli, and said, "Here I am, for you called me." Then Eli perceived that the LORD was calling the boy. Therefore Eli said to Samuel, "Go, lie down; and if he calls you, you shall say, 'Speak, LORD, for your servant is listening.'" So Samuel went and lay down in his place.

Now the LORD came and stood there, calling as before, "Samuel! Samuel!" And Samuel said, "Speak, for your servant is listening." Then the LORD said to Samuel, "See, I am about to do something in Israel that will make both ears of anyone who hears of it tingle. On that day I will fulfill against Eli all that I have spoken concerning his house, from beginning to end. For I have told him that I am about to punish his house, for the iniquity that he knew, because his sons were blaspheming God, and he did not restrain them."

Samuel lay there until morning; then he opened the doors of the house of the LORD. Samuel was afraid to tell the vision to Eli. But Eli called Samuel and said, "Samuel, my son." He said, "Here I am." Eli said, "What was it that he told you? Do not hide it from me. May God do so to you and more also, if you hide anything from me of all that he told you." So Samuel told him everything and hid nothing from him. Then he said, "It is the LORD; let him do what seems good to him."

In those days the Philistines mustered for war against Israel, and Israel went out to battle against them. The Philistines drew up in line against Israel, and when the battle was joined, Israel was defeated by the Philistines, who killed about four thousand men on the field of battle.

When the troops came to the camp, the elders of Israel said, "Why has the LORD put us to rout today before the Philistines? Let us bring the ark of the covenant of the LORD here from Shiloh, so that he may come among us and save us from the power of our enemies." So the people sent to Shiloh, and brought from there the ark of the covenant of the LORD of hosts. The two sons of Eli, Hophni and Phinehas, were there with the ark of the covenant of God.

When the ark of the covenant of the LORD came into the camp, all Israel gave a mighty shout, so that the earth resounded. When the Philistines heard the noise of the shouting, they said, "What does this great shouting in the camp of the Hebrews mean?"

When they learned that the ark of the LORD had come to the camp, the Philistines were afraid; for they said, "Gods have come into the camp." They also said, "Woe to us! For nothing like this has happened before. Woe to us! Who can deliver us from the power of these mighty gods? These are the gods who struck the Egyptians with every sort of plague in the wilderness. Take courage, and be men, O Philistines, in order not to become slaves to the Hebrews as they have been to you; be men and fight."

So the Philistines fought; Israel was defeated, and they fled, everyone to his home. There was a very great slaughter, for there fell of Israel thirty thousand foot soldiers. The ark of God was captured; and the two sons of Eli, Hophni and Phinehas, died.

A man of Benjamin ran from the battle line, and came to Shiloh the same day, with his clothes torn and with earth upon his head. When he arrived, Eli was sitting upon his seat by the road watching, for his heart trembled for the ark of God. When the man came into the city and told the news, all the city cried out.

When Eli heard the sound of the outcry, he said, "What is this uproar?" Then the man came quickly and told Eli. Now Eli was ninety-eight years old and his eyes were set, so that he could not see. The man said to Eli, "I have just come from the battle; I fled from the battle today." He said, "How did it go, my son?" The messenger replied, "Israel has fled before the Philistines, and there has also been a great slaughter among the troops; your two sons also, Hophni and Phinehas, are dead, and the ark of God has been captured." When he mentioned the ark of God, Eli fell over backward from his seat by the side of the gate and he died. He had judged Israel forty years.

Samuel judged Israel all the days of his life. He went on a circuit year by year to Bethel, Gilgal, and Mizpah; and he judged Israel in all these places. Then he would come back to Ramah, for his home was there; he administered justice there to Israel, and built there an altar to the LORD.

King Saul

Saul Becomes King

There was a man of Benjamin whose name was Kish, a man of wealth. He had a son whose name was Saul. There was not a man among the people of Israel more handsome than he; he stood head and shoulders above everyone else.

Now the donkeys of Kish had strayed. So Kish said to his son Saul, "Take one of the boys with you; go and look for the donkeys." He passed through the hill country of Ephraim and Shalishah, but they did not find them.

Saul said to the boy who was with him, "Let us turn back, or my father will stop worrying about the donkeys and worry about us." But he said to him, "There is a man of God in this town. He is a man held in honor. Whatever he says always comes true. Perhaps he will tell us about the journey on which we have set out." As they were entering the town, they saw Samuel coming out toward them.

Now the day before Saul came, the LORD had revealed to Samuel: "Tomorrow about this time I will send to you a man from the land of Benjamin, and you shall anoint him to be ruler over my people Israel. He shall save my people from the hand of the Philistines; for I have seen the suffering of my people, because their outcry has come to me." When Samuel saw Saul, the LORD told him, "Here is the man of whom I spoke to you. He it is who shall rule over my people."

Then Saul approached Samuel inside the gate, and said, "Tell me, please, where is the house of the seer?" Samuel answered Saul, "I am the seer; today you shall eat with me, and in the morning I will tell you all that is on your mind. As for your donkeys that were lost three days ago, give no further thought to them, for they have been found. And on whom is all Israel's desire fixed, if not on you and on all your ancestral house?" Saul answered, "I am only a Benjaminite, from the least of the tribes of Israel, and my family is the humblest of all the families of the tribe of Benjamin. Why then have you spoken to me in this way?"

So Saul ate with Samuel that day. At the break of dawn Samuel called to Saul, "Get up, so that I may send you on your way."

As they were going to the outskirts of the town, Samuel said to Saul, "Tell the boy to go on before us, and stop here yourself for a while, that I may make known to you the word of God."

Samuel took a vial of oil and poured it on his head, and kissed him; he said, "The LORD has anointed you ruler over his people Israel. You shall reign over the people of the LORD and you will save them from the hand of their enemies all around."

As he turned away to leave Samuel, God gave him another heart. A band of prophets met him; and the spirit of God possessed him, and he fell into a prophetic frenzy along with them. When his prophetic frenzy had ended, he went home.

Saul's uncle said to him, "Where did you go?" And he replied, "To seek the donkeys; and when we saw they were not to be found, we went to Samuel."

Saul's uncle said, "Tell me what Samuel said to you."

Saul said to his uncle, "He told us that the donkeys had been found." But about the kingship, of which Samuel had spoken,

he did not tell him anything.

Later Samuel summoned the people and said to them, "Do you see the one whom the LORD has chosen? There is no one like him among all the people." And all the people shouted, "Long live the king!"

Saul's Downfall

Samuel said to Saul, "Thus says the LORD of hosts, 'I will punish the Amalekites for opposing the Israelites when they came up out of Egypt. Now go and attack Amalek, and utterly destroy all that they have.'"

So Saul summoned the people, and defeated the Amalekites. But the people spared the best of the sheep and cattle, and all that was valuable.

The word of the LORD came to Samuel: "I regret that I made Saul king, for he has not carried out my commands." When Samuel came to Saul, Saul said to him, "I have carried out the command of the LORD." But Samuel said, "What then is this bleating of sheep in my ears, and the lowing of cattle that I hear?" Saul said, "They have brought them from the Amalekites; for the people spared the best of the sheep and the cattle, to sacrifice to the LORD your God."

Samuel said, "The LORD said, 'Go, utterly destroy the Amalekites.' Why then did you not obey the voice of the LORD? Why

did you swoop down on the spoil?" Saul said to Samuel, "I have gone on the mission on which the LORD sent me. But from the spoil the people took sheep and cattle, to sacrifice to the LORD." And Samuel said,

> "Has the LORD as great delight
> in burnt offerings and sacrifices,
>   as in obeying the voice of the LORD?
> Surely, to obey is better than sacrifice,
>   and to heed than the fat of rams.
> Because you have rejected the word of the LORD,
>   he has also rejected you from being king."

Saul said to Samuel, "I have sinned. Now therefore, I pray, pardon my sin, and return with me, so that I may worship the LORD." Samuel said to Saul, "I will not return with you; for you have rejected the word of the LORD, and the LORD has rejected you from being king over Israel." As Samuel turned to go away, Saul caught hold of the hem of his robe, and it tore. And Samuel said to him, "The LORD has torn the kingdom of Israel from you this very day, and has given it to a neighbor of yours."

David Sings for Saul

The LORD said to Samuel, "How long will you grieve over Saul? I have rejected him from being king over Israel. Fill your horn with oil and set out; I will send you to Jesse the Bethlehemite, for I have provided for myself a king among his sons." Samuel said, "If Saul hears of it, he will kill me." And the LORD said, "Take a heifer with you, and say, 'I have come to sacrifice to the LORD.'" Samuel did what the LORD commanded, and came to Bethlehem. And he sanctified Jesse and his sons and invited them to the sacrifice.

When they came, he looked on Eliab and thought, "Surely the LORD's anointed is now before the LORD." But the LORD said to Samuel, "Do not look on his appearance or his stature, for the LORD does not see as mortals see; they look on the outward appearance, but the LORD looks on the heart." Then Jesse called Abinadab, and made him pass before Samuel. He said, "Neither has the LORD chosen this one." Jesse made seven of his sons pass before Samuel, and Samuel said to Jesse, "The LORD has not chosen any of these."

Samuel said to Jesse, "Are all your sons here?" And he said, "There remains yet the youngest, but he is keeping the sheep." And Samuel said to Jesse, "Send and bring him." He sent and brought him in. Now he was ruddy, and handsome. The LORD said, "This is the one." Then Samuel took the horn of oil, and anointed him in the presence of his brothers; and the spirit of the LORD came mightily upon David from that day forward.

Now the spirit of the LORD departed from Saul, and an evil spirit tormented him. And Saul's servants said to him, "An evil spirit from God is tormenting you. Let our lord look for someone

who is skillful in playing the lyre; and when the evil spirit from God is upon you, he will play it, and you will feel better." One of the young men answered, "I have seen a son of Jesse the Bethlehemite who is skillful in playing, a man of valor, a warrior, prudent in speech, and a man of good presence; and the LORD is with him."

So Saul sent messengers to Jesse, and said, "Send me your son David who is with the sheep."

And David came to Saul, and entered his service. Saul loved him greatly, and he became his armor-bearer. Whenever the evil spirit came upon Saul, David took the lyre and played it, and Saul would be relieved and feel better, and the evil spirit would depart from him.

David knew many songs, and he wrote many himself. One of the best known is the twenty-third psalm:

The LORD is my shepherd, I shall not want.

He makes me lie down in green pastures;
he leads me beside still waters;
he restores my soul.
He leads me in right paths
for his name's sake.
Even though I walk through the darkest valley,
I fear no evil;
for you are with me;
your rod and your staff—
they comfort me.
You prepare a table before me
in the presence of my enemies;
you anoint my head with oil;
my cup overflows.
Surely goodness and mercy shall follow me
all the days of my life,
and I shall dwell in the house of the LORD
my whole life long.

Another favorite is Psalm 27:

The LORD is my light and my salvation;
whom shall I fear?
The LORD is the stronghold of my life;
of whom shall I be afraid?
When evildoers assail me
to devour my flesh—
my adversaries and foes—
they shall stumble and fall.
Though an army encamp against me,
my heart shall not fear;
though war rise up against me,
yet I will be confident.

106

David and Goliath

Now the Philistines gathered their armies for battle. Saul and the Israelites gathered and formed ranks against the Philistines. And there came out from the camp of the Philistines a champion named Goliath, whose height was six cubits and a span. He had a helmet of bronze on his head, and he was armed with a coat of mail. He had greaves of bronze on his legs and a javelin of bronze slung between his shoulders. The shaft of his spear was like a weaver's beam, and his spear's head weighed six hundred shekels of iron.

He stood and shouted to the ranks of Israel, "Choose a man for yourselves, and let him come down to me. If he is able to fight with me and kill me, then we will be your servants; but if I prevail against him and kill him, then you shall be our servants and serve us." When Saul and all Israel heard these words of the Philistine, they were dismayed and greatly afraid.

For forty days the Philistine came forward and took his stand, morning and evening.

Meanwhile, Jesse said to his son David, "Take this parched grain and these ten loaves, and carry them to the camp to your brothers." Now they were fighting with the Philistines. David left the sheep with a keeper, and went as Jesse had commanded him. He came to the encampment and went and greeted his brothers. As he talked with them, Goliath came up out of the ranks of the Philistines, and spoke the same words as before.

The Israelites said, "Have you seen this man who has come up? The king will greatly enrich the man who kills him, and will give him his daughter and make his family free in Israel." David said to the men who stood by him, "Who is this uncircumcised Philistine that he should defy the armies of the living God?"

His eldest brother Eliab heard him talking to the men; and Eliab's anger was kindled against David. He said, "Why have you come down? With whom have you left those few sheep in the wilderness? I know your presumption and the evil of your heart; for you have come down just to see the battle." David said, "What have I done now? It was only a question."

When the words that David spoke were heard, they repeated them before Saul; and he sent for him. David said to Saul, "Let no one's heart fail; your servant will go and fight with this Philistine." Saul said to David, "You are not able to go against this Philistine; for you are just a boy, and he has been a warrior from his youth."

But David said to Saul, "Your servant used to keep sheep for his father; and whenever a lion or a bear came, and took a lamb from the flock, I went after it and struck it down, rescuing the lamb from its mouth; and if it turned against me, I would catch it by the jaw, strike it down, and kill it. Your servant has killed both lions and bears; and this uncircumcised Philistine shall be like one of them, since he has defied the armies of the living God. The LORD, who saved me from the lion and the bear, will save me from this Philistine." So Saul said to David, "Go, and may the LORD be with you!"

Saul clothed David with his armor; he put a bronze helmet on his head and clothed him with a coat of mail. David strapped Saul's sword over the armor, and he tried in vain to walk, for he was not used to them.

Then David said to Saul, "I cannot walk with these; for I am not used to them." So David removed them. Then he took his staff in his hand, and chose five smooth stones from the wadi, and put them in his shepherd's bag; his sling was in his hand, and he drew near to the Philistine.

When the Philistine saw David, he said, "Am I a dog, that you come to me with sticks?" And the Philistine cursed David by his gods. The Philistine said to David, "Come to me, and I will give your flesh to the birds of the air and to the wild animals of the field."

But David said to the Philistine, "You come to me with sword and spear and javelin; but I come to you in the name of the LORD of hosts, the God of the armies of Israel, whom you have defied. This very day the LORD will deliver you into my hand, so that all the earth may know that there is a God in Israel, and that all this assembly may know that the LORD does not save by sword and spear."

When the Philistine drew nearer to meet David, David put his hand in his bag, took out a stone, slung it, and struck the Philistine on his forehead; the stone sank into his forehead, and he fell face down on the ground.

When the Philistines saw that their champion was dead, they fled. The troops of Israel and Judah rose up with a shout and pursued the Philistines.

Saul took David that day and would not let him return to his father's house. David went out and was successful wherever Saul sent him; as a result, Saul set him over the army. And all the people, even the servants of Saul, approved.

David Fools Saul

As they were coming home, the women came out of all the towns of Israel, singing and dancing, to meet King Saul, with tambourines, with songs of joy, and with musical instruments. And the women sang to one another,

> "Saul has killed his thousands,
>   and David his ten thousands."

Saul was very angry. He said, "They have ascribed to David ten thousands, and to me they have ascribed thousands; what more can he have but the kingdom?" So Saul eyed David from that day on.

The next day an evil spirit from God rushed upon Saul, and he raved within his house, while David was playing the lyre, as he did day by day. Saul had his spear in his hand; and Saul threw the spear, for he thought, "I will pin David to the wall." But David eluded him twice.

Now Saul's daughter Michal loved David. Saul was told, and the thing pleased him. Saul thought, "Let me give her to him that she may be a snare for him and that the hand of the Philistines may be against him." Therefore Saul said to David, "You shall now be my son-in-law." And David said, "Does it seem to you a little thing to become the king's son-in-law, seeing that I am a poor man and of no repute?" Then Saul said, "The king desires no marriage present except that he may be avenged on the king's enemies." Now Saul planned to make David fall by the hand of the Philistines.

When his servants told David these words, David was well pleased to be the king's son-in-law. Before the time had expired, David rose and went, along with his men, and killed one hundred of the Philistines. Saul gave him his daughter Michal as a wife. But when Saul realized that the LORD was with David, and that Saul's daughter Michal loved him, Saul was still more afraid of David. So Saul was David's enemy from that time forward.

Saul sent messengers to David's house to keep watch over him, planning to kill him in the morning. David's wife Michal told him, "If you do not save your life tonight, tomorrow you will be killed." So Michal let David down through the window; he fled away and escaped. Michal took an idol and laid it on the bed; she put a net of goats' hair on its head, and covered it with the clothes.

When Saul sent messengers to take David, she said, "He is sick."

Then Saul sent the messengers to see David for themselves. He said, "Bring him up to me in the bed, that I may kill him." When the messengers came in, the idol was in the bed, with the covering of goats' hair on its head. Saul said to Michal, "Why have you deceived me like this, and let my enemy go, so that he has escaped?"

Saul Pursues David

David left there and escaped to the cave of Adullam; when his brothers and all his father's house heard of it, they went down there to him. Everyone who was in distress, and everyone who was in debt, and everyone who was discontented gathered to him; and he became captain over them. Those who were with him numbered about four hundred.

Saul and his men went to search for him. When David was told, he stayed in the wilderness. When Saul heard that, he pursued David into the wilderness. David was hurrying to get away from Saul, while Saul and his men were closing in on David and his men.

Saul encamped on the hill of Hachilah. David learned that Saul had arrived. So David and Abishai went to the army by night; there Saul lay sleeping within the encampment, with his spear stuck in the ground at his head; and Abner and the army lay around him. Abishai said to David, "God has given your enemy into your hand today; now therefore let me pin him to the ground with one stroke of the spear."

But David said to Abishai, "Do not destroy him; for who can raise his hand against the LORD's anointed, and be guiltless?" David said, "The LORD will strike him down; or his day will come to die; or he will go down into battle and perish. The LORD forbid that I should raise my hand against the LORD's anointed; but now take the spear that is at his head, and the water jar, and let us go." So David took the spear and the water jar, and they went away. No one saw it, for they were all asleep.

Then David stood on top of a hill far away. David called to the army and to Abner, saying, "Abner! Will you not answer?"

Then Abner replied, "Who are you that calls to the king?"

David said to Abner, "Why then have you not kept watch over your lord the king? For one of the people came in to destroy your lord the king. As the LORD lives, you deserve to die, because you have not kept watch over your lord, the LORD's anointed. See now, where is the king's spear, or the water jar that was at his head?"

Saul recognized David's voice, and said, "Is this your voice, my son David?" David said, "It is my voice, my lord, O king." And he added, "Why does my lord pursue his servant? For what have I done? For the king of Israel has come out to seek a single flea, like one who hunts a partridge in the mountains."

Then Saul said, "I have done wrong; come back, my son David, for I will never harm you again, because my life was precious in your sight today."

David replied, "The LORD gave you into my hand today, but I would not raise my hand against the LORD's anointed. As your life was precious today in my sight, so may my life be precious in the sight of the LORD, and may he rescue me from all tribulation." Then Saul said to David, "Blessed be you, my son David!"

Saul Dies

Samuel died, and all Israel mourned for him and buried him in Ramah, his own city. *Now* Saul had expelled the mediums and the wizards from the land. *Then* the Philistines assembled, and came and encamped at Shunem. When Saul saw the army of the Philistines, he was afraid, and his heart trembled greatly. When Saul inquired of the LORD, the LORD did not answer him. Then Saul said to his servants, "Seek out for me a woman who is a medium, so that I may go to her and inquire of her." His servants said to him, "There is a medium at Endor."

So Saul disguised himself and put on other clothes and went there, he and two men with him. They came to the woman by night. And he said, "Consult a spirit for me, and bring up for me the one whom I name to you."

The woman said to him, "Surely you know what Saul has done, how he has cut off the mediums and the wizards from the land. Why then are you laying a snare for my life to bring about my death?" But Saul swore to her by the LORD, "As the LORD lives, no punishment shall come upon you for this thing." Then the woman said, "Whom shall I bring up for you?" He answered, "Bring up Samuel for me."

When the woman saw Samuel, she cried out with a loud voice; and the woman said to Saul, "Why have you deceived me? You are Saul!" The king said to her, "Have no fear; what do you see?" The woman said to Saul, "I see a divine being coming up out of the ground." He said to her, "What is his appearance?" She said, "An old man is coming up; he is wrapped in a robe." So Saul knew that it was Samuel, and he bowed with his face to the ground.

Then Samuel said to Saul, "Why have you disturbed me by bringing me up?" Saul answered, "I am in great distress, for the Philistines are warring against me, and God has turned away from me and answers me no more, so I have summoned you to tell me what I should do." Samuel said, "Why do you ask me, since the LORD has turned from you and become your enemy?

"The LORD has done to you just as he spoke by me; for the LORD has torn the kingdom out of your hand, and given it to your neighbor, David. Because you did not obey the voice of the LORD, and did not carry out his fierce wrath against Amalek, therefore the LORD has done this thing to you today. Moreover the LORD will give Israel along with you into the hands of the Philistines; and tomorrow you and your sons shall be with me; the LORD will also give the army of Israel into the hands of the Philistines."

Immediately Saul fell full length on the ground, filled with fear because of the words of Samuel.

Now the Philistines fought against Israel; and the men of Israel fled before the Philistines. The Philistines overtook Saul and his sons; and the Philistines killed the sons of Saul. The battle pressed hard upon Saul; the archers found him, and he was badly wounded by them. Then Saul said to his armor-bearer, "Draw your sword and thrust me through with it, so that these uncircumcised may not come and thrust me through, and make sport of me." But his armor-bearer was unwilling; for he was terrified. So Saul took his own sword and fell upon it. When his armor-bearer saw that Saul was dead, he also fell upon his sword and died with him.

So Saul and his three sons and his armor-bearer and all his men died together on the same day. When the men of Israel who were on the other side of the valley and those beyond the Jordan saw that the men of Israel had fled and that Saul and his sons were dead, they forsook their towns and fled; and the Philistines came and occupied them.

The next day, when the Philistines came to strip the dead, they found Saul and his three sons fallen on Mount Gilboa. They cut off his head, stripped off his armor, and sent messengers throughout the land of the Philistines to carry the good news to the houses of their idols and to the people. They fastened his body to the wall of Beth-shan. But when the inhabitants of Jabesh-gilead heard what the Philistines had done to Saul, all the valiant men set out, traveled all night long, and took the body of Saul and the bodies of his sons. They came to Jabesh and burned them there. Then they took their bones and buried them.

King David

The Ark Is Returned

There was a long war between the house of Saul and the house of David; David grew stronger and stronger, while the house of Saul became weaker and weaker. Then all the tribes of Israel came to David at Hebron, and they anointed David king over Israel.

Earlier, when the Philistines captured the ark of God, they brought it to Ashdod. The hand of the LORD was heavy upon the people of Ashdod, and he terrified and struck them with tumors. And when the inhabitants of Ashdod saw how things were, they said, "The ark of the God of Israel must not remain with us; let it return to its own place, that it may not kill us and our people."

Then the priests and diviners said, "Get ready a new cart and two milch cows that have never borne a yoke, and yoke the cows to the cart. Take the ark of the LORD and place it on the cart. Then send it off, and let it go its way."

The men did so. The cows went straight to Israel, lowing as they went; they turned neither to the right nor to the left.

Now the people were reaping their wheat. When they looked up and saw the ark, they went with rejoicing to meet it. The cart came into the field and stopped there.

After David became king, he brought up the ark of God to the city of David with rejoicing and with the sound of the trumpet. They brought in the ark of the Lord, and set it inside the tent that David had pitched for it, and David offered burnt offerings before the Lord. When David had finished, he blessed the people.

Moses had given this blessing for the Israelites to use:

The Lord bless you and keep you;
The Lord make his face to shine upon you,
and be gracious to you;
The Lord lift up his countenance upon you,
and give you peace.

As the ark of the LORD came into the city of David, Michal daughter of Saul looked out of the window, and saw King David leaping and dancing before the LORD; and she despised him in her heart.

Then all the people went back to their homes, *and* David returned to bless his household. But Michal the daughter of Saul came out to meet David, and said, "How the king of Israel honored himself today, uncovering himself today before the eyes of his servants' maid, as any vulgar fellow might shamelessly uncover himself!"

David said to Michal, "It was before the LORD, who chose me in place of your father and all his household, to appoint me as prince over Israel, the people of the LORD, that I have danced before the LORD. I will make myself yet more contemptible than this, and I will be abased in my own eyes; but by the maids of whom you have spoken, by them I shall be held in honor."

David Sins

One afternoon, when David was walking about on the roof of the king's house, he saw a woman bathing; the woman was very beautiful. David sent someone to inquire about the woman. It was reported, "This is Bathsheba, the wife of Uriah." So David sent messengers to get her, and she came to him, and he lay with her.

Then she returned to her house. And she sent and told David, "I am pregnant."

So David sent word to Joab *at the battlefield*, "Send me Uriah." When Uriah came to him, David asked how the war was going. Then David said to Uriah, "Go down to your house." But Uriah slept at the entrance of the king's house and did not go to his house. David said to Uriah, "Why did you not go down to your house?" Uriah said, "My lord Joab and the servants of my lord are camping in the open field; shall I then go to my house?" On the next day, David invited him to eat and drink and made him drunk; and in the evening he went out to lie on his couch, but he did not go to his house.

In the morning David wrote a letter to Joab. He wrote, "Set Uriah in the forefront of the hardest fighting, and then draw back from him, so that he may be struck down and die." Joab assigned Uriah to the place where he knew there were valiant warriors. Uriah was killed.

When the wife of Uriah heard that her husband was dead, she made lamentation for him. When the mourning was over, David sent and brought her to his house, and she became his wife, and bore him a son.

But the thing that David had done displeased the LORD, and the LORD sent Nathan to David. He said to him, "There were two men in a certain city, the one rich and the other poor. The rich man had very many flocks and herds; but the poor man had nothing but one little ewe lamb. Now there came a traveler to the rich man, and he was loath to take one of his own flock, but he took the poor man's lamb, and prepared that for the guest who had come to him."

Then David said to Nathan, "The man who has done this deserves to die." Nathan said to David, "You are the man! Thus says the LORD: I anointed you king over Israel, and I rescued you from the hand of Saul; I gave you your master's house, and your master's wives; and if that had been too little, I would have added as much more. Why have you despised the word of the LORD, to do what is evil in his sight? You have struck down Uriah with the sword, and have taken his wife. Therefore the sword shall never depart from your house. Thus says the LORD: I will raise up trouble against you from within your own house; and I will take your wives and give them to your neighbor."

David said to Nathan, "I have sinned against the LORD." Nathan said to David, "The LORD has put away your sin; you shall not die. Nevertheless, because by this deed you have utterly scorned the LORD, the child that is born to you shall die."

The child that Uriah's wife bore to David became very ill. David pleaded with God for the child; David fasted, and lay all night on the ground. On the seventh day the child died. The servants of David were afraid to tell him. But when David saw his servants whispering together, he said to his servants, "Is the child dead?" They said, "He is dead."

Then David rose from the ground, washed, anointed himself, and changed his clothes. He went into the house of the LORD, and worshiped; and they set food before him and he ate. Then his servants said to him, "What is this thing that you have done? You fasted and wept for the child while it was alive; but when the child died, you rose and ate food." He said, "While the child was still alive, I fasted and wept; for I said, 'Who knows? The LORD may be gracious to me, and the child may live.' But now he is dead; why should I fast? Can I bring him back again?"

Then David consoled his wife Bathsheba, and she bore a son, and he named him Solomon.

Absalom Revolts

Now in all Israel there was no one praised so much for his beauty as Absalom; from the sole of his foot to the crown of his head there was no blemish in him. When he cut the hair of his head (for at the end of every year he used to cut it; when it was heavy on him, he cut it), he weighed the hair of his head, two hundred shekels by the king's weight.

Absalom got himself a chariot and horses, and fifty men to run ahead of him. Absolom used to rise early and stand beside the road into the gate; and when anyone brought a suit before the king for judgment, Absalom would call out and say, "From what city are you?" When the person said, "Your servant is of such and such a tribe in Israel," Absalom would say, "See, your claims are good and right; but there is no one deputed by the king to hear you."

Absalom said moreover, "If only I were judge in the land! Then all who had a suit or cause might come to me, and I would give them justice." Whenever people came near to do obeisance to him, he would put out his hand and take hold of them, and kiss them. Thus Absalom did to every Israelite who came to the king for judgment; so Absalom stole the hearts of the people of Israel.

Then Absalom sent secret messengers throughout all the tribes of Israel, saying, "As soon as you hear the sound of the trumpet, then shout: Absalom has become king at Hebron!" The conspiracy grew in strength, and the people with Absalom kept increasing.

A messenger came to David, saying, "The hearts of the Israelites have gone after Absalom."

Then David said to all his officials who were with him at Jerusalem, "Let us flee, or there will be no escape for us from Absalom. Hurry, or he will soon overtake us, and bring disaster down upon us, and attack the city with the edge of the sword."

The king's officials said to the king, "Your servants are ready to do whatever our lord the king decides." So the king left, followed by all his household, except ten concubines whom he left behind to look after the house.

The whole country wept aloud as all the people passed by; the king crossed the Wadi Kidron, and all the people moved on toward the wilderness.

Abiathar came up, and Zadok also, with all the Levites, carrying the ark of the covenant of God. They set down the ark of God, until the people had all passed out of the city. Then the king said to Zadok, "Carry the ark of God back into the city. If I find favor in the eyes of the LORD, he will bring me back and let me see both it and the place where it stays. But if he says, 'I take no pleasure in you,' here I am, let him do to me what seems good to him."

When David came to the summit, where God was worshiped, Hushai the Archite came to meet him with his coat torn and earth on his head. David said to him, "If you go on with me, you will be a burden to me. But if you return to the city and say to Absalom, 'I will be your servant, O king, as I have been your father's servant in time past,' then you will defeat for me the counsel of Ahithophel. The priests Zadok and Abiathar will be with you there. By them you shall report to me everything you hear." So Hushai, David's friend, came into the city, just as Absalom was entering Jerusalem.

David Flees

When David had passed a little beyond the summit, Ziba the servant of Mephibosheth, *Saul's grandson*, met him, with a couple of donkeys saddled, carrying two hundred loaves of bread, one hundred bunches of raisins, one hundred of summer fruits, and one skin of wine. The king said to Ziba, "Why have you brought these?"

Ziba answered, "The donkeys are for the king's household to ride, the bread and summer fruit for the young men to eat, and the wine is for those to drink who faint in the wilderness." Then the king said to Ziba, "All that belonged to Mephibosheth is now yours."

When King David came to Bahurim, a man of the family of the house of Saul came out whose name was Shimei; he came out cursing. He threw stones at David and at all the servants of King David. Shimei shouted, "Out! Out! Murderer! Scoundrel! The Lord has avenged on all of you the blood of the house of Saul, in whose place you have reigned; and the Lord has given

the kingdom into the hand of your son Absalom. See, disaster has overtaken you; for you are a man of blood."

Then Abishai son of Zeruiah said to the king, "Why should this dead dog curse my lord the king? Let me go over and take off his head." But the king said, "My own son seeks my life; how much more now may this Benjaminite! Let him alone, and let him curse; for the LORD has bidden him. It may be that the LORD will look on my distress, and the LORD will repay me with good for this cursing of me today." So David and his men went on the road, while Shimei went along on the hillside opposite him and cursed as he went, throwing stones and flinging dust at him.

Hushai's Advice

Now Absalom and all the Israelites came to Jerusalem; Ahithophel was with him. When Hushai, David's friend, came to Absalom, Hushai said to Absalom, "Long live the king!" Absalom said to Hushai, "Is this your loyalty to your friend?" Hushai said to Absalom, "No; but the one whom the LORD and this people have chosen, his I will be. Just as I have served your father, so I will serve you."

Then Absalom said to Ahithophel, "Give us your counsel; what shall we do?" Now in those days the counsel that Ahithophel gave was as if one consulted the oracle of God.

Ahithophel said to Absalom, "Let me choose twelve thousand men, and I will set out and pursue David tonight. I will come upon him while he is weary and discouraged, and throw him into a panic; and all the people who are with him will flee." The advice pleased Absalom and all the elders of Israel.

Then Absalom said, "Call Hushai also, and let us hear what he has to say."

Then Hushai said to Absalom, "This time the counsel that Ahithophel has given is not good." Hushai continued, "You know that your father and his men are warriors, and that they are enraged, like a bear robbed of her cubs in the field. Besides, your father is expert in war; he will not spend the night with the troops. And when some of our troops fall at the first attack, whoever hears it will say, 'There has been a slaughter among the troops who follow Absalom.' Then even the valiant warrior will utterly melt with fear." Absalom and all the men of Israel said, "The counsel of Hushai is better than the counsel of Ahithophel." For the LORD had ordained to defeat the good counsel of Ahithophel.

Then Hushai said to the priests Zadok and Abiathar, "Send quickly and tell David, 'Do not lodge tonight at the fords of the wilderness, but by all means cross over; otherwise the king and all the people who are with him will be swallowed up.'" So David and the people with him crossed the Jordan.

Absalom Is Caught

Then David mustered the men who were with him into three groups under the command of Joab, Abishai, and Ittai. The king ordered Joab and Abishai and Ittai, saying, "Deal gently for my sake with the young man Absalom."

So the army went out into the field against Israel; and the men of Israel were defeated by the servants of David.

Absalom was riding on his mule, and the mule went under the thick branches of a great oak. His head caught fast in the oak, and he was left hanging between heaven and earth, while the mule went on. A man saw it, and told Joab, "I saw Absalom hanging in an oak." Joab said to the man who told him, "What, you saw him! Why then did you not strike him there to the ground? I would have been glad to give you ten pieces of silver and a belt."

But the man said to Joab, "Even if I felt in my hand the weight of a thousand pieces of silver, I would not raise my hand against

the king's son; for in our hearing the king commanded you and Abishai and Ittai, saying: For my sake protect the young man Absalom!" Joab said, "I will not waste time like this with you." He took three spears in his hand, and thrust them into the heart of Absalom, while he was still alive in the oak.

Then Joab sounded the trumpet, and the troops came back from pursuing Israel. They took Absalom, threw him into a great pit in the forest, and raised over him a very great heap of stones. Then Joab said to a Cushite, "Go, tell the king what you have seen." The Cushite bowed before Joab, and ran.

When the Cushite came to David he said, "Good tidings for my lord the king! For the LORD has vindicated you this day, delivering you from the power of all who rose up against you." The king said to the Cushite, "Is it well with the young man Absalom?" The Cushite answered, "May the enemies of my lord the king, be like that young man."

The king went up to the chamber over the gate, and wept. He said, "O my son Absalom, my son, my son Absalom! Would I had died instead of you, O Absalom, my son, my son!"

It was told Joab, "The king is weeping for Absalom." So the victory that day was turned into mourning. The troops stole into the city as soldiers who are ashamed when they flee in battle. Then Joab came to the king, and said, "Today you have covered with shame the faces of all your officers who have saved your life today, and the lives of your sons and your daughters, and your wives. Commanders and officers are nothing to you; for I perceive that if Absalom were alive and all of us were dead today, then you would be pleased. So go out at once and speak kindly to your servants; for I swear by the LORD, if you do not go, not a man will stay with you this night; and this will be worse for you than any disaster that has come upon you from your youth until now."

Then the king got up and took his seat in the gate. The troops were all told, "See, the king is sitting in the gate"; and all the troops came before the king.

Meanwhile, all the people were disputing throughout all the tribes of Israel, saying, "The king delivered us from the hand of our enemies; and now he has fled out of the land because of Absalom. But Absalom, whom we anointed over us, is dead in battle. Now therefore why do you say nothing about bringing the king back?" And they sent word to the king, "Return, both you and all your servants." So the king came back to the Jordan; and Judah came to meet the king and to bring him over the Jordan.

David Makes Solomon King

King David was old and advanced in years. David said, "Summon to me the priest Zadok, the prophet Nathan, and Benaiah." When they came, the king said to them, "Have my son Solomon ride on my own mule to Gihon. There anoint him king over Israel. Let him enter and sit on my throne; he shall be king in my place."

So Zadok, Nathan, and Benaiah had Solomon ride on King David's mule, and led him to Gihon. There the priest Zadok anointed Solomon. Then they blew the trumpet, and all the people said, "Long live King Solomon!" And all the people went up following him, playing on pipes and rejoicing with great joy.

Then David slept with his ancestors, and was buried in the

city of David. So Solomon sat on the throne of his father David; and his kingdom was firmly established.

The LORD appeared to Solomon in a dream by night; and God said, "Ask what I should give you."

And Solomon said, "O LORD my God, you have made your servant king in place of my father David, although I am only a little child. And your servant is in the midst of the people whom you have chosen, a great people, so numerous they cannot be numbered or counted. Give your servant therefore an under-

standing mind to govern your people, able to discern between good and evil."

It pleased the LORD that Solomon had asked this. God said to him, "Because you have asked this, and have not asked for yourself long life or riches, or for the life of your enemies, but have asked for yourself understanding to discern what is right, I now do according to your word. Indeed I give you a wise and discerning mind; no one like you has been before you and no one like you shall arise after you. I give you also what you have not asked, both riches and honor all your life. If you will walk in my ways, keeping my statutes and my commandments, as your father David walked, then I will lengthen your life."

King Solomon

Solomon Builds the Temple

Now King Hiram of Tyre sent his servants to Solomon, when he heard that they had anointed him king in place of his father; for Hiram had always been a friend to David. Solomon sent word to Hiram, saying, "You know that my father David could not build a house for the name of the LORD his God because of the warfare with which his enemies surrounded him. But now the LORD my God has given me rest on every side. So I intend to build a house for the name of the LORD my God. Therefore command that cedars from the Lebanon be cut for me. There is no one who knows how to cut timber like the Sidonians."

When Hiram heard the words of Solomon, he rejoiced greatly, and said, "Blessed be the LORD today, who has given to David a wise son to be over this great people." Hiram sent word to Solomon, "I will fulfill all your needs in the matter of cedar and cypress timber." So Solomon's builders and Hiram's builders prepared the timber and the stone to build the house.

The inner sanctuary he prepared to set there the ark of the covenant of the LORD. Solomon overlaid the inside of the house with pure gold. Next he overlaid the whole house with gold, in order that the whole house might be perfect.

Now King Solomon invited and received Hiram from Tyre. He was full of skill and knowledge in working bronze.

He cast two pillars of bronze. Then he made the molten sea; it was round, and stood on twelve oxen. Hiram also made the pots, the shovels, and the basins.

Thus all the work on the house of the LORD was finished. Solomon brought in the things that his father David had dedicated, the silver, the gold, and the vessels, and stored them in the treasuries of the house of the LORD.

Then Solomon stood before the altar of the LORD and spread

out his hands to heaven. He said, "O LORD, God of Israel, there is no God like you in heaven above or on earth beneath, keeping covenant and steadfast love for your servants who walk before you with all their heart.

"But will God indeed dwell on the earth? Even heaven and the highest heaven cannot contain you, much less this house that I have built! Hear the plea of your servant and of your people Israel when they pray toward this place.

"If they sin against you—for there is no one who does not sin—and repent, saying, 'We have sinned, and have done wrong'; then hear their prayer and forgive your people who have sinned against you."

When Solomon finished this prayer, he stood and blessed all the assembly of Israel:

"Blessed be the LORD, who has given rest to his people Israel according to all that he promised. The LORD our God be with us, as he was with our ancestors; may he not leave us or abandon us, but incline our hearts to him, to walk in all his ways, and to keep his commandments, so that all the peoples of the earth may know that the LORD is God; there is no other."

Solomon's Wisdom

Later, two women came to the king. The one woman said, "Please, my lord, this woman and I live in the same house; and I gave birth. On the third day after I gave birth, this woman also gave birth. Then this woman's son died in the night. She got up and took my son from beside me while your servant slept. She laid him at her breast, and laid her dead son at my breast. When I rose in the morning to nurse my son, I saw that he was dead; but when I looked at him closely, clearly it was not the son I had borne." But the other woman said, "No, the living son is mine, and the dead son is yours." So they argued before the king.

Then the king said, "Bring me a sword," and they brought a sword. The king said, "Divide the living boy in two; then give half to the one, and half to the other."

But the woman whose son was alive said to the king, "Please, my lord, give her the living boy; certainly do not kill him!" The other said, "It shall be neither mine nor yours; divide it."

Then the king responded: "Give the first woman the living boy. She is his mother." All Israel heard of the judgment that the king had rendered; and they stood in awe of the king, because they perceived that the wisdom of God was in him, to execute justice.

When the queen of Sheba heard of the fame of Solomon, she came to test him with hard questions. She came to Jerusalem with a very great retinue, with camels bearing spices, and very much gold, and precious stones. Solomon answered all her questions; there was nothing hidden from the king that he could not

explain to her. When the queen of Sheba had observed all the wisdom of Solomon, she said, "The report was true that I heard in my own land of your accomplishments and of your wisdom, but I did not believe the reports until I came and my own eyes had seen it. Blessed be the LORD your God, who has delighted in you and set you on the throne of Israel! Because the LORD loved Israel forever, he has made you king to execute justice and righteousness."

134

Solomon's Proverbs

God gave Solomon very great wisdom, discernment, and breadth of understanding, so that Solomon's wisdom surpassed the wisdom of all the people of the east. He composed three thousand proverbs, and his songs numbered a thousand and five.

Here are some proverbs used by the Israelites:

Go to the ant, you lazybones;
   consider its ways, and be wise.

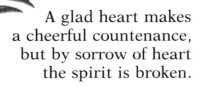

A glad heart makes
a cheerful countenance,
but by sorrow of heart
the spirit is broken.

Better is a dinner of vegetables
   where love is
than a fatted ox
   and hatred with it.

Like clouds and wind without rain
is one who boasts
of a gift never given.

135

Whoever digs a pit
will fall into it.

The mouths of fools are their ruin,
  and their lips a snare to themselves.

When you make a vow to God, do not delay fulfilling it; for
he has no pleasure in fools. Fulfill what you vow.

The lover of money will
not be satisfied with money;
nor the lover of wealth,
with gain.

Do not be quick to anger,
  for anger lodges in the bosom of fools.

Jeroboam

The man Jeroboam was very able, and when Solomon saw that the young man was industrious he gave him charge over all the forced labor of the house of Joseph. About that time, when Jeroboam was leaving Jerusalem, the prophet Ahijah found him on the road. The two of them were alone in the open country when Ahijah laid hold of the new garment he was wearing and tore it into twelve pieces.

He then said to Jeroboam: Take for yourself ten pieces; for thus says the LORD, the God of Israel, "See, I am about to tear the kingdom from the hand of Solomon, and will give you ten tribes. One tribe will remain his, for the sake of my servant David and for the sake of Jerusalem, the city that I have chosen out of all the tribes of Israel. This is because he has forsaken me, and has not walked in my ways, doing what is right in my sight and keeping my statutes and my ordinances. Nevertheless I will not take the whole kingdom away from him but will make him ruler all the days of his life, for the sake of my servant David.

"But I will take the kingdom away from his son and give it to you—that is, the ten tribes. You shall reign over Israel. If you will listen to all that I command you, walk in my ways, and do

what is right in my sight by keeping my statutes and my commandments, as David my servant did, I will be with you, and will build you an enduring house."

Solomon sought therefore to kill Jeroboam; but Jeroboam promptly fled to Egypt until the death of Solomon.

The Kingdom Divides

Solomon slept with his ancestors and was buried in the city of his father David; and his son Rehoboam succeeded him. When Jeroboam heard of it, he returned from Egypt. Jeroboam and all the assembly of Israel came and said to Rehoboam, "Your father made our yoke heavy. Now therefore lighten the hard service that he placed on us, and we will serve you." He said to them, "Go away for three days, then come again to me."

Then King Rehoboam took counsel with the older men who had attended his father Solomon, saying, "How do you advise me to answer this people?" They answered him, "If you will be a servant to this people and speak good words to them, then they will be your servants forever."

Then he consulted with the young men who had grown up with him. "What do you advise that we answer this people?" The young men said, "Thus you should say: 'My little finger is thicker than my father's loins. Whereas my father laid on you a heavy yoke, I will add to your yoke.'"

So Jeroboam and all the people came to Rehoboam the third day. The king disregarded the advice that the older men had given him and spoke according to the advice of the young men, "My father made your yoke heavy, but I will add to your yoke; my father disciplined you with whips, but I will discipline you with scorpions."

When all Israel saw that the king would not listen to them, the people answered the king,

> "What share do we have in David?
>   We have no inheritance in the son of Jesse.
> To your tents, O Israel!
>   Look now to your own house, O David."

So Rehoboam reigned over the Israelites who were living in the towns of Judah. When Israel heard that Jeroboam had returned, they made him king over all Israel. There was no one who followed the house of David, except the tribe of Judah alone.

138

The Prophet Elijah

Elijah and the Widow

Ahab son of Omri began to reign over Israel. Ahab did evil in the sight of the LORD. He took as his wife Jezebel daughter of King Ethbaal, and went and served Baal, and worshiped him. Ahab did more to provoke the anger of the LORD than had all the kings of Israel who were before him.

Now Elijah the Tishbite said to Ahab, "As the LORD the God of Israel lives, there shall be neither dew nor rain these years, except by my word." The word of the LORD came to him, saying, "Hide yourself by the Wadi Cherith. You shall drink from the wadi, and I have commanded the ravens to feed you there." So he went and did according to the word of the LORD. The ravens brought him bread and meat in the morning, and bread and

meat in the evening; and he drank from the wadi. But after a while the wadi dried up.

Then the word of the LORD came to him, saying, "Go now to Zarephath, for I have commanded a widow there to feed you." So he went to Zarephath. When he came to the town, a widow was there gathering sticks. He called to her, "Bring me a little water, so that I may drink." As she was going to bring it, he said, "Bring me a morsel of bread."

But she said, "As the LORD your God lives, I have nothing baked, only a handful of meal in a jar, and a little oil in a jug; I am now gathering a couple of sticks, so that I may go home and prepare it for myself and my son, that we may eat it, and die."

Elijah said to her, "Do not be afraid; go and do as you have said; but first make me a little cake of it and bring it to me, and afterwards make something for yourself and your son. For thus says the LORD the God of Israel: The jar of meal will not be emptied and the jug of oil will not fail until the day that the LORD sends rain on the earth." She went and did as Elijah said. The jar of meal was not emptied, neither did the jug of oil fail, according to the word of the LORD.

After this the son of the woman became ill; his illness was so severe that there was no breath left in him. She then said to Elijah, "What have you against me, O man of God? You have come to me to bring my sin to remembrance, and to cause the death of my son!"

But he said to her, "Give me your son." He carried him up into the upper chamber, and laid him on his own bed. He cried out to the LORD, "O LORD my God, have you brought calamity upon the widow with whom I am staying, by killing her son?" Then he stretched himself upon the child three times, and cried out to the LORD, "O LORD my God, let this child's life come into him again."

The life of the child came into him again, and he revived. Elijah took the child and gave him to his mother. "See, your son is alive." So the woman said to Elijah, "Now I know that you are a man of God, and that the word of the LORD in your mouth is truth."

140

A Contest with Baal

The word of the LORD came to Elijah, in the third year of the drought, saying, "Go, present yourself to Ahab; I will send rain on the earth." *Now* the famine was severe in Samaria. Ahab summoned Obadiah, who was in charge of the palace, and said to *him,* "Go through the land to all the springs of water and to all the wadis; perhaps we may find grass to keep the horses and mules alive."

As Obadiah was on the way, Elijah met him. Obadiah said, "Is it you, my lord Elijah?" He answered him, "It is I. Go, tell your lord that Elijah is here."

And he said, "How have I sinned, that you would hand your servant over to Ahab, to kill me? There is no nation to which my lord has not sent to seek you. But now you say, 'Go, tell your lord that Elijah is here.' As soon as I have gone, the spirit of the LORD will carry you I know not where; so, when Ahab cannot find you, he will kill me."

Elijah said, "I will show myself to him today." So Obadiah went, and told Ahab.

When Ahab saw Elijah, Ahab said to him, "Is it you, you troubler of Israel?" He answered, "I have not troubled Israel; but you have, because you have forsaken the commandments of the LORD and followed the Baals. Now therefore have all Israel assemble for me at Mount Carmel, with the four hundred fifty prophets of Baal."

So Ahab assembled the prophets at Mount Carmel. Elijah then came near to all the people, and said, "How long will you go limping with two different opinions? If the LORD is God, follow him; but if Baal, then follow him." The people did not answer him a word. Then Elijah said to the people, "I, even I only, am left a prophet of the LORD; but Baal's prophets number four hundred fifty. Let two bulls be given to us; let them choose one bull for themselves, cut it in pieces, and lay it on the wood, but put no fire to it; I will prepare the other bull. Then you call on the name of your god and I will call on the name of the LORD; the god who answers by fire is indeed God."

142

All the people answered, "Well spoken!"

Then the prophets of Baal took the bull that was given them, prepared it, and called on the name of Baal from morning until noon, crying, "O Baal, answer us!" But there was no answer.

At noon Elijah mocked them, saying, "Cry aloud! Surely he is a god; either he is meditating, or he has wandered away, or he

is on a journey, or perhaps he is asleep and must be awakened." Then they cried aloud and, as was their custom, they cut themselves with swords and lances until the blood gushed out over them. They raved on until the time of the offering of the oblation, but there was no response.

Then Elijah said to all the people, "Come closer to me"; and all the people came closer to him. First he repaired the altar of the LORD that had been thrown down. Elijah took twelve stones, *and* built an altar. Then he made a trench around the altar. Next he put the wood in order, cut the bull in pieces, and laid it on the wood. He said, "Fill four jars with water and pour it on the burnt offering and on the wood." Then he said, "Do it a second time." Again he said, "Do it a third time," so that the water ran all around the altar, and filled the trench also with water.

At the time of the offering of the oblation, the prophet Elijah came near and said, "O LORD, God of Abraham, Isaac, and Israel, let it be known this day that you are God in Israel, that I am your servant, and that I have done all these things at your bidding. Answer me, O LORD, answer me, so that this people may know that you, O LORD, are God, and that you have turned their hearts back." Then the fire of the LORD fell and consumed the burnt offering, the wood, the stones, and the dust, and even licked up the water that was in the trench. When all the people saw it, they fell on their faces and said, "The LORD indeed is God." Elijah said to them, "Seize the prophets of Baal; do not let one of them escape." Then they seized them.

Elijah said to Ahab, "Go up, eat and drink; for there is a sound of rushing rain." Elijah said to his servant, "Look toward the sea." He looked, and said, "There is nothing." Then he said, "Go again seven times." At the seventh time he said, "A little cloud no bigger than a person's hand is rising out of the sea." Then he said, "Go say to Ahab, 'Harness your chariot and go down before the rain stops you.'" In a little while the heavens grew black with clouds and wind; there was a heavy rain. Ahab rode off and went to Jezreel. But the hand of the LORD was on Elijah; he girded up his loins and ran in front of Ahab to the entrance of Jezreel.

Elijah Hides

Ahab told Jezebel all that Elijah had done, and how he had killed all the prophets of Baal. Then Jezebel sent a messenger to Elijah, saying, "So may the gods do to me, and more also, if I do not make your life like the life of one of them by this time tomorrow." Then he was afraid; he got up and fled for his life.

He sat down under a broom tree *and said*, "It is enough; now, O Lord, take away my life." Then he lay down and fell asleep.

Suddenly an angel touched him and said to him, "Get up and eat." He looked, and there was a cake baked on hot stones, and a jar of water. He ate and drank, and lay down again.

The angel of the Lord came a second time, touched him, and said, "Get up and eat, otherwise the journey will be too much for you." He got up, and ate and drank; then he went in the strength of that food forty days and forty nights to Horeb the mount of God. At that place he came to a cave, and spent the night there.

Then the word of the Lord came to him, saying, "Go out and stand on the mountain, for the Lord is about to pass by." Now there was a wind, so strong that it was splitting mountains and breaking rocks in pieces, but the Lord was not in the wind; and

145

after the wind an earthquake, but the LORD was not in the earthquake; and after the earthquake a fire, but the LORD was not in the fire; and after the fire a sound of sheer silence.

Then there came a voice to him that said, "What are you doing here, Elijah?"

He answered, "I have been very zealous for the LORD, the God of hosts; for the Israelites have forsaken your covenant, thrown down your altars, and killed your prophets with the sword. I alone am left, and they are seeking my life."

Then the LORD said to him, "Return to Damascus; you shall anoint Hazael as king over Aram. Also you shall anoint Jehu as king over Israel; and you shall anoint Elisha as prophet in your place. Yet I will leave seven thousand in Israel, all the knees that have not bowed to Baal."

Naboth's Vineyard

Naboth had a vineyard in Jezreel, beside the palace of King Ahab. And Ahab said to Naboth, "Give me your vineyard, so that I may have it for a vegetable garden, because it is near my house; I will give you a better vineyard for it; or, if it seems good to you, I will give you its value in money." But Naboth said to Ahab, "The LORD forbid that I should give you my ancestral inheritance." Ahab went home resentful and sullen because of what Naboth the Jezreelite had said. He lay down on his bed, turned away his face, and would not eat.

His wife Jezebel came to him and said, "Why are you so depressed that you will not eat?" He said to her, "Because I spoke to Naboth and said to him, 'Give me your vineyard for money; or else, if you prefer, I will give you another vineyard for it'; but he answered, 'I will not give you my vineyard.'" His wife Jezebel said to him, "Do you now govern Israel? Get up, eat some food, and be cheerful; I will give you the vineyard of Naboth."

So she wrote letters in Ahab's name and sealed them with his seal; she sent the letters to the elders and the nobles. She wrote, "Proclaim a fast, and seat Naboth at the head of the assembly; seat two scoundrels opposite him, and have them bring a charge against him, saying, 'You have cursed God and the king.' Then take him out, and stone him to death." The men of his city, the elders and the nobles who lived in his city, did as Jezebel had sent word to them. Then they sent to Jezebel, saying, "Naboth has been stoned; he is dead."

As soon as Jezebel heard that Naboth was dead, Jezebel said to Ahab, "Go, take possession of the vineyard of Naboth for Naboth is dead." Ahab set out to go down to the vineyard of Naboth to take possession of it.

Then the word of the LORD came to Elijah, saying: Go down to meet King Ahab. He is now in the vineyard of Naboth, where he has gone to take possession. You shall say to him, "Thus says the LORD: Have you killed, and also taken possession? In the place where dogs licked up the blood of Naboth, dogs will also lick up your blood."

Ahab said to Elijah, "Have you found me, O my enemy?" He answered, "I have found you. Because you have sold yourself to do what is evil in the sight of the LORD, I will bring disaster on you; I will consume you, because you have provoked me to anger and have caused Israel to sin. Concerning Jezebel the LORD said, 'The dogs shall eat Jezebel within the bounds of Jezreel.'"

When Ahab heard those words, he tore his clothes and put sackcloth over his bare flesh; he fasted, lay in the sackcloth, and went about dejectedly. Then the word of the LORD came to Elijah: "Have you seen how Ahab has humbled himself before me? Because he has humbled himself before me, I will not bring the disaster in his days; but in his son's days I will bring the disaster on his house."

Jezebel's End

King Jehoshaphat of Judah came down to *Ahab* the king of Israel. *Ahab* said to his servants, "Do you know that Ramoth-gilead belongs to us, yet we are doing nothing to take it out of the hand of the king of Aram?" He said to Jehoshaphat, "Will you go with me to battle at Ramoth-gilead?" Jehoshaphat replied, "I am as you are; my people are your people, my horses are your horses."

Ahab said to Jehoshaphat, "I will disguise myself and go into battle, but you wear your robes." Now the king of Aram had commanded, "Fight with no one small or great, but only with the king of Israel." When the captains of the chariots saw Jehoshaphat, they said, "It is surely the king of Israel." So they turned to fight against him; and Jehoshaphat cried out. When the captains of the chariots saw that it was not the king of Israel, they turned back from pursuing him.

But a certain man drew his bow and unknowingly struck *Ahab*. So he said to the driver of his chariot, "Turn around, and carry me out of the battle, for I am wounded." At evening he died; the blood from the wound had flowed into the bottom of the chariot. The dogs licked up his blood, according to the word of the LORD.

Joram, son of Ahab, became king over Israel. Then Jehu conspired against Joram. Jehu mounted his chariot and went to Jezreel, where Joram was. In Jezreel, the sentinel spied Jehu arriving. Joram said, "Take a horseman; send him to meet them, and let him say, 'Is it peace?'" So the horseman went to meet him; he said, "Thus says the king, 'Is it peace?'" Jehu responded, "What have you to do with peace? Fall in behind me." The sentinel reported, saying, "The messenger reached them, but he is not coming back."

Then King Joram went to meet Jehu. When Joram saw Jehu, he said, "Is it peace, Jehu?" He answered, "What peace can there be, so long as the many whoredoms and sorceries of your mother Jezebel continue?" Then Joram reined about and fled, saying, "Treason!" Jehu drew his bow and shot Joram and he sank in his chariot. Jehu said, "Lift him out, and throw him on the plot of ground belonging to Naboth the Jezreelite; for remember how the LORD uttered this oracle against him: 'For the blood of Naboth and for the blood of his children, says the LORD, I swear I will repay you on this very plot of ground.' Now therefore lift him out and throw him on the plot of ground, in accordance with the word of the LORD."

When Jehu came to Jezreel, Jezebel heard of it; she painted her eyes, and adorned her head, and looked out of the window. As Jehu entered the gate, she said, "Is it peace, murderer of your master?" He looked up to the window and said, "Who is on my side? Who?" Two or three eunuchs looked out at him. He said, "Throw her down." So they threw her down; some of her blood spattered on the wall and on the horses, which trampled on her. Then he went in and ate and drank; he said, "See to that cursed woman and bury her; for she is a king's daughter." But when they went to bury her, they found no more of her than the skull and the feet and the palms of her hands. When they came back and told him, he said, "This is the word of the LORD, which he spoke by his servant Elijah, 'In the territory of Jezreel the dogs shall eat the flesh of Jezebel.'"

Elijah Goes to Heaven

The LORD said to *Elijah*, "You shall anoint Elisha as prophet in your place."

So he found Elisha, who was plowing. There were twelve yoke of oxen ahead of him. Elijah passed by him and threw his mantle over him. He left the oxen, ran after Elijah, and said, "Let me kiss my father and my mother, and then I will follow you." Then *Elisha* took the yoke of oxen, and slaughtered them; using the equipment from the oxen, he boiled their flesh, and gave it to the people, and they ate. Then he set out and followed Elijah, and became his servant.

Now when the LORD was about to take Elijah up to heaven by a whirlwind, Elijah and Elisha were on their way from Gilgal. Elijah said to Elisha, "Stay here; for the LORD has sent me as far as Bethel." But Elisha said, "As the LORD lives, and as you yourself live, I will not leave you."

So they went down to Bethel. The company of prophets who were in Bethel came out to Elisha, and said to him, "Do you know that today the LORD will take your master away from you?" And he said, "Yes, I know."

Elijah said to him, "Elisha, stay here; for the LORD has sent me to Jericho." But he said, "As the LORD lives, and as you yourself live, I will not leave you." So they came to Jericho. The company of prophets who were at Jericho drew near to Elisha, and said to him, "Do you know that today the LORD will take your master away from you?" And he answered, "Yes, I know; be silent."

Then Elijah said to him, "Stay here; for the LORD has sent me to the Jordan." But he said, "As the LORD lives, and as you yourself live, I will not leave you." So the two of them went on. As they both were standing by the Jordan, Elijah took his mantle, rolled it up, and struck the water; the water was parted to the one side and to the other, until the two of them crossed on dry ground.

When they had crossed, Elijah said to Elisha, "Tell me what I may do for you, before I am taken from you." Elisha said, "Please let me inherit a double share of your spirit." He responded, "You have asked a hard thing; yet, if you see me as I am being taken from you, it will be granted you; if not, it will not."

150

As they continued walking and talking, a chariot of fire and horses of fire separated the two of them, and Elijah ascended in a whirlwind into heaven.

Elisha kept watching and crying out, "Father, father! The chariots of Israel and its horsemen!" But when he could no longer see him, he grasped his own clothes and tore them in two pieces.

He picked up the mantle of Elijah that had fallen from him, and went back and stood on the bank of the Jordan. He took the mantle of Elijah and struck the water. The water was parted to the one side and to the other, and Elisha went over.

When the company of prophets who were at Jericho saw him at a distance, they declared, "The spirit of Elijah rests on Elisha."

Elisha and Naaman

Naaman, commander of the army of the king of Aram, was a great man and in high favor with his master. The man, though a mighty warrior, suffered from leprosy. Now the Arameans on one of their raids had taken a young girl captive from the land of Israel, and she served Naaman's wife. She said to her mistress, "If only my lord were with the prophet who is in Samaria! He would cure him of his leprosy." So Naaman told his lord what the girl from the land of Israel had said. And the king of Aram said, "Go then, and I will send along a letter to the king of Israel."

He went, taking with him ten talents of silver, six thousand shekels of gold, and ten sets of garments. He brought the letter to the king of Israel, which read, "When this letter reaches you, know that I have sent to you my servant Naaman, that you may cure him of his leprosy."

When the king of Israel read the letter, he tore his clothes and said, "Am I God, to give death or life, that this man sends word to me to cure a man of his leprosy? Just look and see how he is trying to pick a quarrel with me."

But when Elisha the man of God heard that the king of Israel had torn his clothes, he sent a message to the king, "Why have you torn your clothes? Let him come to me, that he may learn that there is a prophet in Israel." So Naaman came with his horses and chariots, and halted at the entrance of Elisha's house. Elisha sent a messenger to him, saying, "Go, wash in the Jordan seven times, and your flesh shall be restored and you shall be clean."

But Naaman became angry and went away, saying, "I thought that for me he would surely come out, and stand and call on the name of the LORD his God, and would wave his hand over the spot, and cure the leprosy! Are not Abana and Pharpar, the rivers of Damascus, better than all the waters of Israel? Could I not wash in them, and be clean?" He turned and went away in a rage.

But his servants approached and said to him, "Father, if the prophet had commanded you to do something difficult, would you not have done it? How much more, when all he said to you was, 'Wash, and be clean'?" So he went down and immersed himself seven times in the Jordan, according to the word of the man of God; his flesh was restored like the flesh of a young boy, and he was clean.

Then he returned to the man of God and said, "Now I know that there is no God in all the earth except in Israel; please accept a present from your servant." But he said, "As the LORD lives, whom I serve, I will accept nothing!" He urged him to accept, but he refused. Then Naaman said, "If not, please let two mule-loads of earth be given to your servant; for your servant will no longer offer burnt offering or sacrifice to any god except the LORD. He said to him, "Go in peace."

The Prophets

God Calls Isaiah

After Elisha died, the Lord raised up other prophets to bring his word to the people. One of them was Isaiah, who proclaimed God's message to several kings of Judah. Isaiah described how God called him:

In the year that King Uzziah died, I saw the LORD sitting on a throne, high and lofty; and the hem of his robe filled the temple. Seraphs were in attendance above him; each had six wings: with two they covered their faces, and with two they covered their feet, and with two they flew. And one called to another and said:

"Holy, holy, holy is the LORD of hosts;
the whole earth is full of his glory."

The pivots on the thresholds shook at the voices of those who called, and the house filled with smoke. And I said: "Woe is me! I am lost, for I am a man of unclean lips, and I live among a people of unclean lips; yet my eyes have seen the King, the LORD of hosts!"

Then one of the seraphs flew to me, holding a live coal that had been taken from the altar with a pair of tongs. The seraph touched my mouth with it and said: "Now that this has touched your lips, your guilt has departed and your sin is blotted out." Then I heard the voice of the LORD saying, "Whom shall I send, and who will go for us?"

And I said, "Here am I; send me!"

Isaiah Warns the People

Isaiah spoke out strongly against greed and injustice:

The LORD said:
Because the daughters of Zion are haughty
   and walk with outstretched necks,
   glancing wantonly with their eyes,
mincing along as they go,
   tinkling with their feet;
the LORD will afflict with scabs
   the heads of the daughters of Zion.

In that day the LORD will take away the finery of the anklets, the headbands, and the crescents; the pendants, the bracelets, and the scarfs; the festal robes, the mantles, the cloaks, and the handbags.

Instead of perfume there will be a stench;
   and instead of a sash, a rope;
and instead of well-set hair, baldness;
   and instead of a rich robe, a binding of sackcloth;
   instead of beauty, shame.
Ah, you who join house to house,
   who add field to field,
until there is room for no one but you.
The LORD of hosts has sworn in my hearing:
Surely many houses shall be desolate,
   large and beautiful houses, without inhabitant.
Ah, you who rise early in the morning
   in pursuit of strong drink,
whose feasts consist of lyre and harp,
   tambourine and flute and wine,
but who do not regard the deeds of the LORD,
   or see the work of his hands!
Therefore my people go into exile without knowledge;
   their nobles are dying of hunger,
   and their multitude is parched with thirst.

The Lord Gives a Sign

But the people did not listen to Isaiah, and the ills he foretold came to pass.

In the days of Ahaz, king of Judah, King Rezin of Aram and King Pekah of Israel went up to attack Jerusalem. The heart of Ahaz and the heart of his people shook as the trees of the forest shake before the wind.

Then the LORD said to Isaiah, Go out to meet Ahaz and say to him, Take heed, be quiet, do not fear, and do not let your heart be faint because of these two smoldering stumps of firebrands *who have* plotted evil against you. It shall not stand, and it shall not come to pass.

Again the LORD spoke to Ahaz, saying, Ask a sign of the LORD your God. But Ahaz said, I will not ask, and I will not put the LORD to the test. Then Isaiah said: "Therefore the LORD himself will give you a sign. Look, the young woman is with child and shall bear a son, and shall name him Immanuel. Before the child knows how to refuse the evil and choose the good, the land before whose two kings you are in dread will be deserted."

Isaiah made other prophecies of good to come:
The people who walked in darkness
   have seen a great light.
For a child has been born for us,
   a son given to us;
authority rests upon his shoulders;
   and he is named
Wonderful Counselor, Mighty God,
   Everlasting Father, Prince of Peace.
His authority shall grow continually,
   and there shall be endless peace
for the throne of David and his kingdom.
   He will establish and uphold it
with justice and with righteousness
   from this time onward and forevermore.
The zeal of the LORD of hosts will do this.

Jeremiah Prophesies

At a later time God appointed Jeremiah to be his prophet and to call the rulers and people of Judah to repent.

The LORD *said to Jeremiah*: Go and buy a potter's earthenware jug. Go out to the valley of the son of Hinnom and proclaim there the words that I tell you. You shall say: Thus says the LORD of hosts, the God of Israel: I am going to bring such disaster upon this place that the ears of everyone who hears of it will tingle. Because the people have forsaken me, and have profaned this place by making offerings in it to other gods whom neither they nor their ancestors nor the kings of Judah have known; and because they have filled this place with the blood of the innocent, and gone on building the high places of Baal to burn their children in the fire as burnt offerings to Baal, which I did not command or decree, nor did it enter my mind.

Therefore the days are surely coming, says the LORD, when this place shall no more be called the valley of the son of Hinnom, but the valley of Slaughter. I will make void the plans of Judah and Jerusalem, and will make them fall by the sword before their enemies. I will give their dead bodies for food to the birds of the air and to the wild animals of the earth. And I will make this city a horror; everyone who passes by it will be horrified and will hiss because of all its disasters.

Then you shall break the jug in the sight of those who go with you, and shall say to them: Thus says the LORD of hosts: So will I break this people and this city, as one breaks a potter's vessel, so that it can never be mended.

And the houses of Jerusalem and the houses of the kings of Judah shall be defiled—all the houses upon whose roofs offerings have been made to the whole host of heaven, and libations have been poured out to other gods.

Jeremiah stood in the court of the LORD's house and said to all the people: Thus says the LORD of hosts, the God of Israel: I am now bringing upon this city and upon all its towns all the disaster that I have pronounced against it, because they have stiffened their necks, refusing to hear my words.

Now the priest Pashhur, who was chief officer in the house of the LORD, heard Jeremiah prophesying these things. Then Pashhur struck the prophet Jeremiah, and put him in the stocks that were in the house of the LORD.

The next morning Jeremiah said to him, The LORD has named you not Pashhur but "Terror-all-around." For thus says the LORD: I am making you a terror to yourself and to all your friends; and they shall fall by the sword of their enemies while you look on. And I will give all Judah into the hand of the king of Babylon. I will give all the wealth of this city, all its prized belongings, and all the treasures of the kings of Judah into the hand of their enemies, who shall seize them, and carry them to Babylon. And you, Pashhur, and all who live in your house, shall go into captivity, to Babylon. There you shall die, and there you shall be buried, you and all your friends, to whom you have prophesied falsely.

The King Burns Jeremiah's Scroll

In the fourth year of King Jehoiakim of Judah, this word came to Jeremiah from the LORD: Take a scroll and write on it all the words that I have spoken to you against Israel and Judah. It may be that when the house of Judah hears of all the disasters that I intend to do to them, all of them may turn from their evil ways, so that I may forgive their iniquity and their sin.

Then Jeremiah called Baruch, and Baruch wrote on a scroll at Jeremiah's dictation all the words of the LORD. And Jeremiah ordered Baruch, saying, "I am prevented from entering the house of the LORD; so you read the words of the LORD from the scroll in the hearing of all the people of Judah. It may be that all of them will turn from their evil ways, for great is the anger and wrath that the LORD has pronounced against this people."

Then Baruch read the words of Jeremiah from the scroll in the house of the LORD.

When Micaiah heard all the words of the LORD from the scroll, he went down to the king's house. All the officials were sitting there: Micaiah told them all the words that he had heard.

Then all the officials sent to Baruch, and said, "Bring the scroll that you read and come." So Baruch came to them. And they said to him, "Sit down and read it to us."

So Baruch read it to them. When they heard all the words, they turned to one another in alarm, and said to Baruch, "We certainly must report all these words to the king."

Then the officials said to Baruch, "Go and hide, you and Jeremiah, and let no one know where you are."

They went and reported all the words to the king. Then the king sent Jehudi to get the scroll, and Jehudi read it to the king. Now the king was sitting in his winter apartment, and there was a fire burning in the brazier before him. As Jehudi read three or four columns, the king would cut them off with a penknife and throw them into the fire until the entire scroll was consumed. Neither the king, nor any of his servants who heard all these words, was alarmed. And the king commanded them to arrest Baruch and Jeremiah. But the LORD hid them.

After the king had burned the scroll, the word of the LORD came to Jeremiah: Take another scroll and write on it all the former words that were in the first scroll. And concerning King Jehoiakim you shall say: Thus says the LORD, You have dared to burn this scroll. Therefore thus says the LORD concerning King Jehoiakim: He shall have no one to sit upon the throne of David, and his dead body shall be cast out to the heat by day and the frost by night. And I will punish him and his offspring and his servants for their iniquity; I will bring on them all the disasters with which I have threatened them—but they would not listen.

Then Jeremiah took another scroll and Baruch wrote on it at Jeremiah's dictation all the words of the scroll that King Jehoiakim of Judah had burned in the fire; and many similar words were added to them.

Jeremiah Is Arrested

Zedekiah *became king of Judah*. But neither he nor his servants nor the people of the land listened to the words of the LORD that he spoke through the prophet Jeremiah.

Yet King Zedekiah sent Jehucal and the priest Zephaniah to the prophet Jeremiah saying, "Please pray for us to the LORD our God."

Meanwhile, the army of Pharaoh had come out of Egypt; and when the Chaldeans who were besieging Jerusalem heard news of them, they withdrew from Jerusalem.

Then the word of the LORD came to the prophet Jeremiah: Thus says the LORD, God of Israel: This is what the two you shall say to the king of Judah who sent you to inquire of me, Pharaoh's army, which set out to help you, is going to return to its own land, to Egypt. And the Chaldeans shall return and fight against this city; they shall take it and burn it with fire.

Thus says the LORD: Do not deceive yourselves, saying, "The Chaldeans will surely go away from us," for they will not go away. Even if you defeated the whole army of Chaldeans who are fighting against you, and there remained of them only wounded men in their tents, they would rise up and burn this city with fire.

Now when the Chaldean army had withdrawn from Jerusalem at the approach of Pharaoh's army, Jeremiah set out from Jerusalem to go to the land of Benjamin to receive his share of property among the people there. When he reached the Benjamin Gate, a sentinel named Irijah arrested the prophet Jeremiah saying, "You are deserting to the Chaldeans." And Jeremiah said, "That is a lie; I am not deserting to the Chaldeans." But Irijah would not listen to him, and brought him to the officials. The officials were enraged at Jeremiah, and they beat him and imprisoned him in the house of the secretary Jonathan, for it had been made a prison.

Then King Zedekiah sent for him. The king questioned him secretly in his house, and said, "Is there any word from the LORD?" Jeremiah said, "There is!" Then he said, "You shall be handed over to the king of Babylon."

Jeremiah also said to King Zedekiah, "What wrong have I done to you or your servants or this people, that you have put me in prison? Where are your prophets who prophesied to you, saying, 'The king of Babylon will not come against you and against this land'? Now please hear me, my lord king: do not send me back to the house of the secretary Jonathan to die there."

So King Zedekiah gave orders, and they committed Jeremiah to the court of the guard; and a loaf of bread was given him daily from the bakers' street, until all the bread of the city was gone.

Rescued from a Cistern

Now Shephatiah, Gedaliah, Jucal, and Pashhur heard the words that Jeremiah was saying to all the people: Thus says the Lord, those who stay in this city shall die by the sword, by famine, and by pestilence; but those who go out to the Chaldeans shall live; they shall have their lives as a prize of war, and live. Thus says the Lord, This city shall surely be handed over to the army of the king of Babylon and be taken.

Then the officials said to the king, "This man ought to be put to death, because he is discouraging the soldiers who are left in this city, and all the people, by speaking such words to them. For this man is not seeking the welfare of this people, but their harm."

King Zedekiah said, "Here he is; he is in your hands; for the king is powerless against you." So they took Jeremiah and threw him into the cistern of Malchiah, the king's son, which was in the court of the guard, letting Jeremiah down by ropes. Now there was no water in the cistern, but only mud, and Jeremiah sank in the mud.

Ebed-melech the Ethiopian, a eunuch in the king's house, heard that they had put Jeremiah into the cistern. The king happened to be sitting at the Benjamin Gate, so Ebed-melech left the king's

house and spoke to the king, "My lord king, these men have acted wickedly in all they did to the prophet Jeremiah by throwing him into the cistern to die there of hunger, for there is no bread left in the city."

Then the king commanded Ebed-melech, "Take three men with you from here, and pull the prophet Jeremiah up from the cistern before he dies." So Ebed-melech took the men with him and went to the house of the king, to a wardrobe of the storehouse, and took from there old rags and worn-out clothes, which he let down to Jeremiah in the cistern by ropes. Then Ebed-melech the Ethiopian said to Jeremiah, "Just put the rags and clothes between your armpits and the ropes." Jeremiah did so. Then they drew Jeremiah up by the ropes and pulled him out of the cistern.

And Jeremiah remained in the court of the guard until the day that Jerusalem was taken.

Daniel Interprets Strange Writing

In the third year of the reign of King Jehoiakim of Judah, King Nebuchadnezzar of Babylon came to Jerusalem and besieged it. The LORD let King Jehoiakim of Judah fall into his power.

Then the king *of Babylon* commanded his palace master to bring some of the Israelites of the royal family and of the nobility, young men without physical defect and handsome, versed in every branch of wisdom, endowed with knowledge and insight, and competent to serve in the king's palace; they were to be taught the literature and language of the Chaldeans. The king assigned them a daily portion of the royal rations of food and wine. They were to be educated for three years, so that at the end of that time they could be stationed in the king's court. Among them was Daniel.

King Belshazzar, *who succeeded Nebuchadnezzar*, made a great festival for a thousand of his lords, and he was drinking wine in the presence of the thousand. Belshazzar commanded that they bring in the vessels of gold and silver that his father Nebuchadnezzar had taken out of the temple in Jerusalem so that the king and his lords, his wives, and his concubines might drink from them. They drank wine and praised the gods of gold and silver, bronze, iron, wood, and stone.

Immediately the fingers of a human hand appeared and began writing on the wall. Then the king's face turned pale, and his knees knocked together. The king cried, "Whoever can read this writing and tell me its interpretation shall be clothed in purple, have a chain of gold around his neck, and rank third in the kingdom." Then all the king's wise men came in, but they could not read the writing.

The queen heard the discussion of the king and his lords. The queen said, "Do not let your thoughts terrify you or your face grow pale. There is a man in your kingdom who is endowed with a spirit of the holy gods. In the days of your father he was found to have wisdom like the wisdom of the gods. Let Daniel be called, and he will give the interpretation."

Then Daniel was brought in before the king. The king said to Daniel, "I have heard that you can give interpretations and solve problems. Now if you are able to read the writing and tell me its interpretation, you shall be clothed in purple, have a chain of gold around your neck, and rank third in the kingdom."

Then Daniel answered, "Give your rewards to someone else! Nevertheless I will read the writing to the king and let him know the interpretation. O king, the Most High God gave your father Nebuchadnezzar kingship, greatness, glory, and majesty. But when his spirit was hardened so that he acted proudly, he was deposed, and his glory was stripped from him. He was driven from human society, and his mind was made like that of an animal until he learned that the Most High God has sovereignty over the kingdom of mortals.

"And you, Belshazzar his son, have not humbled your heart, even though you knew all this! You have exalted yourself against the LORD of heaven! The vessels of his temple have been brought in and you have been drinking wine from them. You have praised

the gods of silver and gold; but the God in whose power is your very breath, and to whom belong all your ways, you have not honored.

"So from his presence the hand was sent and this writing was inscribed. And this is the writing that was inscribed: MENE, MENE, TEKEL, and PARSIN. This is the interpretation of the matter: MENE, God has numbered the days of your kingdom and brought it to an end; TEKEL, you have been weighed on the scales and found wanting; PERES, your kingdom is divided and given to the Medes and Persians."

That very night Belshazzar was killed. And Darius the Mede received the kingdom.

In the Lion's Den

It pleased Darius to set over the kingdom one hundred twenty satraps, and over them three presidents, including Daniel. Soon Daniel distinguished himself above all the other presidents, and the king planned to appoint him over the whole kingdom. So the presidents and the satraps tried to find grounds for complaint against Daniel. But they could find no grounds for complaint or any corruption. The men said, "We shall not find any ground for complaint against this Daniel unless we find it in connection with the law of his God."

So the presidents and satraps came to the king and said, "O King Darius, live forever! All the presidents of the kingdom are agreed that the king should establish an ordinance, that whoever prays to anyone, divine or human, for thirty days, except to you, O king, shall be thrown into a den of lions. Now, O king, sign the document, so that it cannot be changed." Therefore King Darius signed the document.

Although Daniel knew that the document had been signed, he continued to get down on his knees three times a day to pray to his God and praise him.

The conspirators came and found Daniel praying. Then they approached the king and said, "O king! Did you not sign an interdict, that anyone who prays to anyone, divine or human, within thirty days except to you, O king, shall be thrown into a den of lions? Daniel pays no attention to you, O king, but he is saying his prayers three times a day."

When the king heard the charge, he was very much distressed. He was determined to save Daniel, and until the sun went down he made every effort to rescue him. Then the conspirators came to the king and said to him, "Know, O king, that it is a law of the Medes and Persians that no interdict or ordinance that the king establishes can be changed."

Then the king gave the command, and Daniel was thrown into the den of lions. The king said to Daniel, "May your God, whom you faithfully serve, deliver you!" Then the king went to his palace and spent the night fasting.

At break of day, the king hurried to the den of lions. He cried out anxiously, "O Daniel, servant of the living God, has your God been able to deliver you from the lions?"

Daniel then said, "O king, live forever! My God sent his angel and shut the lions' mouths so that they would not hurt me, because I was found blameless before him."

The king was exceedingly glad and commanded that Daniel be taken up out of the den. And no kind of harm was found on him, because he had trusted in his God.

Return of the Exiles

In the first year of King Cyrus of Persia, in order that the word of the LORD might be accomplished, *Cyrus* declared:

"The LORD, the God of heaven, has charged me to build him a house at Jerusalem in Judah. Any of those among you who are of his people are now permitted to go up to Jerusalem and rebuild the house of the LORD."

The families of Judah and Benjamin, and the priests and the Levites—everyone whose spirit God had stirred—got ready to go up and rebuild the house of the LORD in Jerusalem. All their neighbors aided them.

The people gathered in Jerusalem. Then Jeshua and Zerubbabel set out to build the altar of God *and* rebuild the house of God; and with them were the prophets of God, helping them. They finished their building in the sixth year of the reign of King Darius.

The people of Israel celebrated the dedication of this house of God with joy. On the fourteenth day of the first month the returned exiles kept the passover. They killed the passover lamb for all the returned exiles, for their fellow priests, and for themselves. It was eaten also by all who had joined them and separated themselves from the pollutions of the nations of the land to worship the LORD, the God of Israel. With joy they celebrated the festival of unleavened bread seven days; for the LORD had made them joyful, and had turned the heart of the king of Assyria to them, so that he aided them in the work on the house of the God of Israel.

Job's Troubles

There was once a man in the land of Uz whose name was Job. That man was blameless and upright, one who feared God and turned away from evil. There were born to him seven sons and three daughters.

Job would rise early in the morning and offer burnt offerings according to the number of them all; for Job said, "It may be that my children have sinned."

One day the heavenly beings came to present themselves before the Lord, and Satan also came among them. The Lord said to Satan, "Have you considered my servant Job? There is no one like him who fears God and turns away from evil."

Then Satan answered the Lord, "Does Job fear God for nothing? You have blessed the work of his hands, and his possessions have increased in the land. But touch all that he has, and he will curse you to your face."

The Lord said to Satan, "Very well, all that he has is in your power."

One day a messenger came to Job and said, "The oxen were plowing and donkeys were feeding beside them, and the Sabeans fell on them and carried them off, and killed the servants." While he was still speaking another came and said, "The fire of God fell from heaven and burned up the sheep and the servants, and consumed them." While he was still speaking, another came and said, "Your sons and daughters were in their eldest brother's house, and suddenly a great wind came across the desert, struck the four corners of the house, and it fell on the young people, and they are dead."

Then Job fell on the ground and worshiped. He said, "The Lord gave, and the Lord has taken away; blessed be the name of the Lord."

The heavenly beings came *again* to present themselves before the Lord. The Lord said to Satan, "*Job* still persists in his integrity, although you incited me to destroy him."

Then Satan answered the Lord, "All that people have they will give to save their lives. But touch his flesh, and he will curse you."

The Lord said to Satan, "Very well, he is in your power."

So Satan inflicted loathsome sores on Job from the sole of his foot to the crown of his head.

Then his wife said to him, "Curse God, and die."

But he said to her, "Shall we receive the good at the hand of God, and not receive the bad?"

Now when Job's three friends heard of all *his* troubles they met together to go comfort him. When they saw him from a distance, they did not recognize him, and they raised their voices

and wept aloud. They sat with him on the ground seven days and seven nights, and no one spoke a word to him, for they saw that his suffering was very great.

After this Job opened his mouth and cursed the day of his birth.

"Why did I not die at birth,
    come forth from the womb and expire?
Why is light given to one in misery,
    and life to the bitter in soul,
Why is light given to one who cannot see the way,
    whom God has fenced in?
I am not at ease, nor am I quiet;
    I have no rest; but trouble comes."

Then Eliphaz the Temanite answered:
"Think now, who that was innocent ever perished?
    Or where were the upright cut off?
As I have seen, those who plow iniquity
    and sow trouble reap the same.
How happy is the one whom God reproves;
    therefore do not despise the discipline of the Almighty."

Then Job answered:
"Teach me, and I will be silent;
    make me understand how I have gone wrong."

Then Bildad the Shuhite answered:
"Does God pervert justice?
If you are pure and upright,
surely then he will restore to you your rightful place."
Then Job answered:
"I will say to God, Do not condemn me;
let me know why you contend against me."
Then Zophar the Naamathite answered:
"Should a multitude of words go unanswered,
and should one full of talk be vindicated?
Know then that God exacts of you less than your guilt
deserves."
Then Job answered:
"I am a laughingstock to my friends;
I, who called upon God and he answered me,
a just and blameless man, I am a laughingstock."
Then the Lord answered Job out of the whirlwind:
"Who is this that darkens counsel
by words without knowledge?
"Where were you when I laid the foundation of the earth?
Tell me, if you have understanding.
Who determined its measurements—surely you know!
Or who stretched the line upon it?
Or who shut in the sea with doors
when it burst out from the womb?—
Have you commanded the morning since your days began,
and caused the dawn to know its place?
Who has cut a channel for the torrents of rain,
and a way for the thunderbolt?
Can you lift up your voice to the clouds,
so that a flood of waters may cover you?
Is the wild ox willing to serve you?
Will it spend the night at your crib?"
Then Job answered the Lord:
"See, I am of small account; what shall I answer you?
I lay my hand on my mouth.

I have spoken once, and I will not answer;
   twice, but will proceed no further."
I have uttered what I did not understand.
I had heard of you by the hearing of the ear,
   but now my eye sees you;
therefore I despise myself
   and repent in dust and ashes."

After the LORD had spoken these words to Job, the LORD said to Eliphaz, "My wrath is kindled against you and your two friends; for you have not spoken of me what is right. Now therefore offer up a burnt offering; and my servant Job shall pray for you for I will accept his prayer not to deal with you according to your folly; for you have not spoken of me what is right, as my servant Job has done."

And the LORD restored the fortunes of Job when he had prayed for his friends; and the LORD gave Job twice as much as he had before. The LORD blessed the latter days of Job more than his beginning; and he had fourteen thousand sheep, six thousand camels, a thousand yoke of oxen, and a thousand donkeys. He also had seven sons and three daughters. He named the first Jemimah,

the second Keziah,

and the third Keren-happuch.

And Job died, old and full of days.

Jonah

Now the word of the LORD came to Jonah son of Amittai, saying, "Go at once to Nineveh, that great city, and cry out against it; for their wickedness has come up before me." But Jonah set out to flee to Tarshish from the presence of the LORD. He went down to Joppa and found a ship going to Tarshish; so he paid his fare and went on board, to go with them to Tarshish, away from the presence of the LORD.

But the LORD hurled a great wind upon the sea, and such a mighty storm came upon the sea that the ship threatened to break up. Then the mariners were afraid, and each cried to his god. They threw the cargo that was in the ship into the sea, to lighten it for them. Jonah, meanwhile, had gone down into the hold of the ship and had lain down, and was fast asleep. The captain came and said to him, "What are you doing sound asleep? Get up, call on your god! Perhaps the god will spare us a thought so that we do not perish."

The sailors said to one another, "Come, let us cast lots, so that we may know on whose account this calamity has come upon us." So they cast lots, and the lot fell on Jonah. Then they said to him, "Tell us why this calamity has come upon us. What is your occupation? Where do you come from? What is your country? And of what people are you?" "I am a Hebrew," he replied. "I worship the LORD, the God of heaven, who made the sea and the dry land." Then the men were even more afraid, and said to him, "What is this that you have done!" For the men knew that he was fleeing from the presence of the LORD, because he had told them so.

Then they said to him, "What shall we do to you, that the sea may quiet down for us?" For the sea was growing more and more tempestuous. He said to them, "Pick me up and throw me into the sea; then the sea will quiet down for you; for I know it is because of me that this great storm has come upon you." Nevertheless the men rowed hard to bring the ship back to land, but they could not, for the sea grew more and more stormy against them. Then they cried out to the LORD, "Please, O LORD, we pray, do not let us perish on account of this man's life. Do not make us guilty of innocent blood; for you, O LORD, have done as it pleased you." So they picked Jonah up and threw him into the sea; and the sea ceased from its raging. Then the men feared the LORD even more, and they offered a sacrifice to the LORD and made vows.

But the LORD provided a large fish to swallow up Jonah; and Jonah was in the belly of the fish three days and three nights.

Then Jonah prayed to the LORD his God from the belly of the fish, saying,

"I called to the LORD out of my distress,
    and he answered me;

out of the belly of Sheol I cried,
  and you heard my voice.
You cast me into the deep,
  into the heart of the seas,
  and the flood surrounded me;
all your waves and your billows
  passed over me.
The waters closed in over me;
  the deep surrounded me;
weeds were wrapped around my head
  at the roots of the mountains.
As my life was ebbing away,
  I remembered the LORD;
and my prayer came to you,
  into your holy temple.
Those who worship vain idols
  forsake their true loyalty.
But I with the voice of thanksgiving
  will sacrifice to you;
what I have vowed I will pay.
  Deliverance belongs to the LORD!"

Then the LORD spoke to the fish, and it spewed Jonah out upon the dry land.

The word of the LORD came to Jonah a second time, saying, "Get up, go to Nineveh, that great city, and proclaim to it the message that I tell you." So Jonah set out and went to Nineveh, according to the word of the LORD. Now Nineveh was an exceedingly large city, a three days' walk across. Jonah began to go into the city, going a day's walk. And he cried out, "Forty days more, and Nineveh shall be overthrown!" And the people of Nineveh believed God; they proclaimed a fast, and everyone, great and small, put on sackcloth.

When the news reached the king of Nineveh, he rose from his throne, removed his robe, covered himself with sackcloth, and sat in ashes. Then he had a proclamation made in Nineveh: "By the decree of the king and his nobles: No human being or animal, no herd or flock, shall taste anything. They shall not feed, nor shall they drink water. Human beings and animals shall be covered with sackcloth, and they shall cry mightily to God. All shall turn from their evil ways and from the violence that is in their hands. Who knows? God may relent and change his mind; he may turn from his fierce anger, so that we do not perish."

When God saw what they did, how they turned from their evil ways, God changed his mind about the calamity that he had said he would bring upon them; and he did not do it.

But this was very displeasing to Jonah, and he became angry. He prayed to the LORD and said, "O LORD! Is not this what I said while I was still in my own country? That is why I fled to Tarshish at the beginning; for I knew that you are a gracious God and merciful, slow to anger, and abounding in steadfast love, and ready to relent from punishing. And now, O LORD, please take my life from me, for it is better for me to die than to live."

And the LORD said, "Is it right for you to be angry?"

Then Jonah went out of the city and sat down east of the city, and made a booth for himself there. He sat under it in the shade, waiting to see what would become of the city.

The LORD God appointed a bush, and made it come up over Jonah, to give shade over his head, to save him from his discomfort; so Jonah was very happy about the bush. But when dawn came up the next day, God appointed a worm that attacked the bush, so that it withered. When the sun rose, God prepared a sultry east wind, and the sun beat down on the head of Jonah so that he was faint and asked that he might die. He said, "It is better for me to die than to live."

But God said to Jonah, "Is it right for you to be angry about the bush?"

And he said, "Yes, angry enough to die."

Then the LORD said, "You are concerned about the bush, for which you did not labor and which you did not grow; it came into being in a night and perished in a night. And should I not be concerned about Nineveh, that great city, in which there are more than a hundred and twenty thousand persons who do not know their right hand from their left, and also many animals?"

New
Testament
Stories

The Birth, Childhood, and Baptism of Jesus

John Is Born

In the days of King Herod of Judea, there was a priest named Zechariah. His wife was Elizabeth. Both of them were righteous before God, living according to all the commandments of the Lord. But they had no children, and both were getting on in years.

Once when *Zechariah* was serving as priest, he was chosen to enter the sanctuary of the Lord and offer incense. Now at the time of the incense offering, the whole assembly of the people was praying outside. Then there appeared to him an angel of the Lord, standing at the right side of the altar of incense. When Zechariah saw him, he was terrified; and fear overwhelmed him.

But the angel said to him, "Do not be afraid, Zechariah, for your prayer has been heard. Your wife Elizabeth will bear you a son, and you will name him John. You will have joy and gladness, and many will rejoice at his birth, for he will be great in the sight of the Lord. He must never drink wine or strong drink; even before his birth he will be filled with the Holy Spirit. He will turn many of the people of Israel to the Lord their God. With the spirit and power of Elijah he will go before him, to turn the hearts of parents to their children, and the disobedient to the wisdom of the righteous, to make ready a people prepared for the Lord."

Zechariah said to the angel, "How will I know that this is so? For I am an old man, and my wife is getting on in years." The angel replied, "I am Gabriel. I stand in the presence of God, and I have been sent to speak to you and to bring you this good news. But now, because you did not believe my words, which will be fulfilled in their time, you will become mute, unable to speak, until the day these things occur."

Meanwhile the people were waiting for Zechariah, and wondered at his delay in the sanctuary. When he did come out, he could not speak to them, and they realized that he had seen a vision in the sanctuary. He kept motioning to them and remained unable to speak. When his time of service was ended, he went to his home.

Now the time came for Elizabeth to give birth, and she bore a son. Her neighbors and relatives heard that the Lord had shown his great mercy to her, and they rejoiced with her.

On the eighth day they came to circumcise the child, and they were going to name him Zechariah after his father. But his mother said, "No; he is to be called John." They said to her, "None of your relatives has this name." Then they began motioning to his father to find out what name he wanted to give him. He asked for a writing tablet and wrote, "His name is John."

Immediately his mouth was opened and his tongue freed, and he began to speak, praising God. Fear came over all their neighbors, and all these things were talked about throughout the entire hill country of Judea. All who heard them pondered them and said, "What then will this child become?" For, indeed, the hand of the Lord was with him.

An Angel Comes to Mary

The angel Gabriel was sent by God to a town in Galilee called Nazareth, to a virgin engaged to a man whose name was Joseph, of the house of David. The virgin's name was Mary.

And he came to her and said, "Greetings, favored one! The Lord is with you." But she was much perplexed by his words and pondered what sort of greeting this might be. The angel said to her, "Do not be afraid, Mary, for you have found favor with God. And now, you will conceive in your womb and bear a son, and you will name him Jesus. He will be great, and will be called the Son of the Most High, and the Lord God will give to him the throne of his ancestor David. He will reign over the house of Jacob forever, and of his kingdom there will be no end."

Mary said to the angel, "How can this be, since I am a virgin?" The angel said to her, "The Holy Spirit will come upon you, and the power of the Most High will overshadow you; therefore the child to be born will be holy; he will be called Son of God. And now, your relative Elizabeth in her old age has also conceived a son; and this is the sixth month for her who was said to be barren. For nothing will be impossible with God." Then Mary said, "Here am I, the servant of the Lord; let it be with me according to your word." Then the angel departed from her.

Jesus Is Born

 In those days a decree went out from Emperor Augustus that all the world should be registered. This was the first registration and was taken while Quirinius was governor of Syria. All went to their own towns to be registered.

Joseph also went from the town of Nazareth in Galilee to Judea, to the city of David called Bethlehem, because he was descended from the house and family of David. He went to be registered with Mary, to whom he was engaged and who was expecting a child.

While they were there, the time came for her to deliver her child. And she gave birth to her firstborn son and wrapped him in bands of cloth, and laid him in a manger, because there was no place for them in the inn.

In that region there were shepherds living in the fields, keeping watch over their flock by night. Then an angel of the Lord stood before them, and the glory of the Lord shone around them, and they were terrified.

But the angel said to them, "Do not be afraid; for see—I am bringing you good news of great joy for all the people: to you is born this day in the city of David a Savior, who is the Messiah, the Lord. This will be a sign for you: you will find a child wrapped in bands of cloth and lying in a manger."

And suddenly there was with the angel a multitude of the heavenly host, praising God and saying,

"Glory to God in the highest heaven,
   and on earth peace among those whom he favors!"

When the angels had left them and gone into heaven, the shepherds said to one another, "Let us go now to Bethlehem and see this thing that has taken place, which the Lord has made known to us." So they went with haste and found Mary and Joseph, and the child lying in the manger. When they saw this, they made known what had been told them about this child; and all who heard it were amazed at what the shepherds told them.

But Mary treasured all these words and pondered them in her heart.

The shepherds returned, glorifying and praising God for all they had heard and seen, as it had been told them.

A Star Guides the Wise Men

After Jesus was born, wise men from the East came to Jerusalem, asking, "Where is the child who has been born king of the Jews? For we observed his star at its rising, and have come to pay him homage." When King Herod heard this, he was frightened, and all Jerusalem with him; and calling together all the chief priests and scribes of the people, he inquired of them where the Messiah was to be born. They told him, "In Bethlehem of Judea; for so it has been written by the prophet:

'And you, Bethlehem, in the land of Judah,
    are by no means least among the rulers of Judah;
for from you shall come a ruler
    who is to shepherd my people Israel.' "

190

Then Herod secretly called for the wise men and learned from them the exact time when the star had appeared. Then he sent them to Bethlehem, saying, "Go and search diligently for the child; and when you have found him, bring me word so that I may also go and pay him homage."

They set out; and there, ahead of them, went the star that they had seen at its rising, until it stopped over the place where the child was. On entering the house, they saw the child with Mary his mother; and they knelt down and paid him homage. Then, opening their treasure chests, they offered him gifts of gold, frankincense, and myrrh. And having been warned in a dream not to return to Herod, they left for their own country by another road.

After they had left, an angel of the Lord appeared to Joseph in a dream and said, "Get up, take the child and his mother, and flee to Egypt, and remain there until I tell you; for Herod is about to search for the child, to destroy him." Then Joseph got up, took the child and his mother by night, and went to Egypt, and remained there until the death of Herod.

When Herod died, an angel of the Lord appeared to Joseph and said, "Go to the land of Israel, for those who were seeking the child's life are dead." Then Joseph took the child and his mother to Galilee and made his home in Nazareth.

Jesus Is Lost

The child Jesus grew and became strong, filled with wisdom; and the favor of God was upon him.

Now every year his parents went to Jerusalem for the festival of the Passover. When he was twelve years old, they went up as usual. When the festival was ended and they started to return, the boy Jesus stayed behind in Jerusalem, but his parents did not know it. Assuming that he was in the group of travelers, they went a day's journey. Then they started to look for him among their relatives and friends.

When they did not find him, they returned to Jerusalem to search for him. After three days they found him in the temple,

sitting among the teachers, listening to them and asking them questions. And all who heard him were amazed at his understanding and his answers. When his parents saw him they were astonished; and his mother said to him, "Child, why have you treated us like this? Look, your father and I have been searching for you in great anxiety."

He said to them, "Why were you searching for me? Did you not know that I must be in my Father's house?" But they did not understand what he said to them. Then he went with them to Nazareth, and was obedient to them.

John Begins Baptizing

In those days John the Baptist appeared in the wilderness of Judea, proclaiming, "Repent, for the kingdom of heaven has come near." This is the one of whom the prophet Isaiah spoke when he said,

> "The voice of one crying out
>> in the wilderness:
> 'Prepare the way of the Lord,
>> make his paths straight.'"

Now John wore clothing of camel's hair with a leather belt around his waist, and his food was locusts and wild honey. The people of Jerusalem and all Judea were going out to him, and they were baptized by him in the river Jordan, confessing their sins.

John said to the crowds that came out to be baptized by him, "You brood of vipers! Who warned you to flee from the wrath to come? Bear fruits worthy of repentance. Even now the ax is lying at the root of the trees; every tree that does not bear good fruit is cut down and thrown into the fire."

The crowds asked him, "What then should we do?"

In reply he said to them, "Whoever has two coats must share with anyone who has none; and whoever has food must do likewise."

Even tax collectors came to be baptized, and they asked him, "Teacher, what should we do?"

He said to them, "Collect no more than the amount prescribed for you."

Soldiers also asked him, "And we, what should we do?"

He said to them, "Do not extort money from anyone by threats or false accusation, and be satisfied with your wages."

As the people were filled with expectation, and were questioning in their hearts concerning John, whether he might be the Messiah, John answered all of them by saying, "I baptize you with water; but one who is more powerful than I is coming; I am not worthy to untie the thong of his sandals. He will baptize you with the Holy Spirit and fire."

So, with many other exhortations, he proclaimed the good news to the people.

Jesus Is Baptized

Then Jesus came from Galilee to John at the Jordan, to be baptized by him. John would have prevented him, saying, "I need to be baptized by you, and do you come to me?"

But Jesus answered him, "Let it be so now; for it is proper for us in this way to fulfill all righteousness." Then he consented.

And when Jesus had been baptized, just as he came up from the water, suddenly the heavens were opened to him and he saw the Spirit of God descending like a dove and alighting on him. And a voice from heaven said, "This is my Son, the Beloved, with whom I am well pleased."

Then Jesus was led up by the Spirit into the wilderness to be tempted by the devil. He fasted forty days and forty nights, and afterwards he was famished.

The tempter came and said to him, "If you are the Son of God, command these stones to become loaves of bread."

But he answered, "It is written,

'One does not live by bread alone,
    but by every word that comes from the mouth of God.'"

Then the devil took him to the holy city and placed him on the pinnacle of the temple, saying to him, "If you are the Son of God, throw yourself down; for it is written,

'He will command his angels concerning you,'
  and 'On their hands they will bear you up,
so that you will not dash your foot against a stone.' "

Jesus said to him, "Again it is written, 'Do not put the Lord your God to the test.' "

Again, the devil took him to a very high mountain and showed him all the kingdoms of the world and their splendor; and he said to him, "All these I will give you, if you will fall down and worship me." Jesus said to him, "Away with you, Satan! for it is written,

'Worship the Lord your God,
  and serve only him.' "

Then the devil left him, and angels came and waited on him.

Jesus in Galilee

John Is Imprisoned

Herod the ruler, who had been rebuked by John because of all the evil things that Herod had done, added to them all by shutting up John in prison.

When Jesus heard that John had been arrested, he withdrew to Galilee. He left Nazareth and made his home in Capernaum by the sea, in the territory of Zebulun and Naphtali, so that what had been spoken through the prophet Isaiah might be fulfilled:

"Land of Zebulun, land of Naphtali,
  on the road by the sea, across the Jordan, Galilee of the Gentiles—
the people who sat in darkness
  have seen a great light,
and for those who sat in the region and shadow of death
  light has dawned."

From that time Jesus began to proclaim, "Repent, for the kingdom of heaven has come near."

The First Disciples

As Jesus passed along the Sea of Galilee, he saw Simon and his brother Andrew casting a net into the sea—for they were fishermen. And Jesus said to them, "Follow me and I will make you fish for people." And immediately they left their nets and followed him. As he went a little farther, he saw James son of Zebedee and his brother John, who were in their boat mending the nets. Immediately he called them; and they left their father Zebedee in the boat with the hired men, and followed him.

Once while Jesus was standing beside the lake of Gennesaret, and the crowd was pressing in on him to hear the word of God,

he saw two boats there at the shore of the lake. He got into one of the boats, the one belonging to Simon, and asked him to put out a little way from the shore. Then he sat down and taught the crowds from the boat.

When he had finished speaking, he said to Simon, "Put out into the deep water and let down your nets for a catch." Simon answered, "Master, we have worked all night long but have caught nothing. Yet if you say so, I will let down the nets." When they had done this, they caught so many fish that their nets were beginning to break. So they signaled their partners in the other boat to come and help them. And they came and filled both boats, so that they began to sink.

When Simon Peter saw it, he fell down at Jesus' knees, saying, "Go away from me, Lord, for I am a sinful man!" For he and all who were with him were amazed at the catch of fish that they had taken.

Then Jesus said to Simon, "Do not be afraid; from now on you will be catching people."

Jesus Casts Out an Unclean Spirit

They went to Capernaum; and when the sabbath came, Jesus entered the synagogue and taught. They were astounded at his teaching, for he taught them as one having authority, and not as the scribes.

Just then there was in their synagogue a man with an unclean spirit, and he cried out, "What have you to do with us, Jesus of Nazareth? Have you come to destroy us? I know who you are, the Holy One of God."

But Jesus rebuked him, saying, "Be silent, and come out of him!" And the unclean spirit, convulsing him and crying with a loud voice, came out of him.

They were all amazed, and they kept on asking one another, "What is this? A new teaching—with authority! He commands even the unclean spirits, and they obey him." At once his fame began to spread throughout the surrounding region of Galilee.

As soon as they left the synagogue, they entered the house of Simon and Andrew, with James and John. Now Simon's mother-in-law was in bed with a fever, and they told him about her at once. He came and took her by the hand and lifted her up. Then the fever left her, and she began to serve them.

Jesus Heals Leprosy

Once, when he was in one of the cities, there was a man covered with leprosy. When he saw Jesus, he bowed with his face to the ground and begged him, "Lord, if you choose, you can make me clean."

Moved with pity, Jesus stretched out his hand and touched him, and said to him, "I do choose. Be made clean!" Immediately the leprosy left him, and he was made clean.

After sternly warning him he sent him away at once, saying to him, "See that you say nothing to anyone; but go, show yourself to the priest, and offer for your cleansing what Moses commanded, as a testimony to them."

But he went out and began to proclaim it freely, and to spread the word, so that Jesus could no longer go into a town openly, but stayed out in the country; and people came to him from every quarter to hear him and to be cured of their diseases.

But he would withdraw to deserted places and pray.

200

Jesus Picks Twelve Apostles

Jesus went throughout Galilee, teaching in their synagogues and proclaiming the good news of the kingdom and curing every disease and every sickness among the people.

Jesus went out again beside the sea; the whole crowd gathered around him, and he taught them. As he was walking along, he saw Levi son of Alphaeus sitting at the tax booth, and he said to him, "Follow me." And he got up and followed him.

And as he sat at dinner in Levi's house, many tax collectors and sinners were also sitting with Jesus and his disciples—for there were many who followed him. When the scribes of the Pharisees saw that he was eating with sinners and tax collectors, they said to his disciples, "Why does he eat with tax collectors and sinners?"

When Jesus heard this, he said to them, "Those who are well have no need of a physician, but those who are sick. Go and learn what this means, 'I desire mercy, not sacrifice.' For I have come to call not the righteous but sinners."

Now during those days he went out to the mountain to pray; and he spent the night in prayer to God. And when day came, he called his disciples and chose twelve of them, whom he also named apostles: Simon, whom he named Peter, and his brother Andrew, and James, and John, and Philip, and Bartholomew, and Matthew, and Thomas, and James son of Alphaeus, and Simon, who was called the Zealot, and Judas son of James, and Judas Iscariot, who became a traitor.

Then Jesus summoned his twelve disciples and gave them authority over unclean spirits, to cast them out, and to cure every disease and every sickness.

Soon afterwards he went on through cities and villages, proclaiming and bringing the good news of the kingdom of God. The twelve were with him, as well as some women who had been cured of evil spirits and infirmities: Mary, called Magdalene, from whom seven demons had gone out, and Joanna, the wife of Herod's steward Chuza, and Susanna, and many others, who provided for them out of their resources.

The Story of the Lost Sheep

Now all the tax collectors and sinners were coming near to listen to him. And the Pharisees and the scribes were grumbling and saying, "This fellow welcomes sinners and eats with them."

So he told them this parable: "Which one of you, having a hundred sheep and losing one of them, does not leave the ninety-nine in the wilderness and go after the one that is lost until he finds it? When he has found it, he lays it on his shoulders and rejoices. And when he comes home, he calls together his friends and neighbors, saying to them, 'Rejoice with me, for I have found my sheep that was lost.' Just so, I tell you, there will be more joy in heaven over one sinner who repents than over ninety-nine righteous persons who need no repentance."

So again Jesus said to them, "Very truly, I tell you, I am the gate for the sheep. All who came before me are thieves and bandits; but the sheep did not listen to them. I am the gate. Whoever enters by me will be saved, and will come in and go out and find pasture. The thief comes only to steal and kill and destroy. I came that they may have life, and have it abundantly.

"I am the good shepherd. The good shepherd lays down his life for the sheep. The hired hand, who is not the shepherd and does not own the sheep, sees the wolf coming and leaves the sheep and runs away—and the wolf snatches them and scatters them. I am the good shepherd. I know my own and my own know me, just as the Father knows me and I know the Father. And I lay down my life for the sheep. I have other sheep that do not belong to this fold. I must bring them also, and they will listen to my voice. So there will be one flock, one shepherd."

The Centurion's Servant

After Jesus had finished all his sayings in the hearing of the people, he entered Capernaum. A centurion there had a slave whom he valued highly, and who was ill and close to death. When he heard about Jesus, he sent some Jewish elders to him, asking him to come and heal his slave. When they came to Jesus, they appealed to him earnestly, saying, "He is worthy of having you do this for him, for he loves our people, and it is he who built our synagogue for us." And Jesus went with them, but when he was not far from the house, the centurion sent friends to say

to him, "LORD, do not trouble yourself, for I am not worthy to have you come under my roof; therefore I did not presume to come to you. But only speak the word, and let my servant be healed. For I also am a man set under authority, with soldiers under me; and I say to one, 'Go,' and he goes, and to another, 'Come,' and he comes, and to my slave, 'Do this,' and the slave does it." When Jesus heard him, he was amazed and said to those who followed him, "Truly I tell you, in no one in Israel have I found such faith. I tell you, many will come from east and west and will eat with Abraham and Isaac and Jacob in the kingdom of heaven, while the heirs of the kingdom will be thrown into the outer darkness, where there will be weeping and gnashing of teeth." And to the centurion Jesus said, "Go; let it be done for you according to your faith." And the servant was healed in that hour.

The Sower and the Seed

Jesus began to teach them many things in parables, and in his teaching he said to them: "Listen! A sower went out to sow. And as he sowed, some seed fell on the path, and the birds came and ate it up. Other seed fell on rocky ground, where it did not have much soil, and it sprang up quickly, since it had no depth of soil. And when the sun rose, it was scorched; and since it had no root, it withered away. Other seed fell among thorns, and the thorns grew up and choked it, and it yielded no grain. Other seed fell into good soil and brought forth grain, growing up and increasing and yielding thirty and sixty and a hundredfold."

And he said, "Let anyone with ears to hear listen!" Then his disciples asked him what this parable meant. He said, "To you it has been given to know the secrets of the kingdom of God; but to others I speak in parables, so that 'looking they may not perceive, and listening they may not understand.'

"Now the parable is this: The seed is the word of God. The ones on the path are those who have heard; then the devil comes and takes away the word from their hearts, so that they may not believe and be saved. The ones on the rock are those who, when they hear the word, receive it with joy. But these have no root; they believe only for a while and in a time of testing fall away. As for what fell among the thorns, these are the ones who

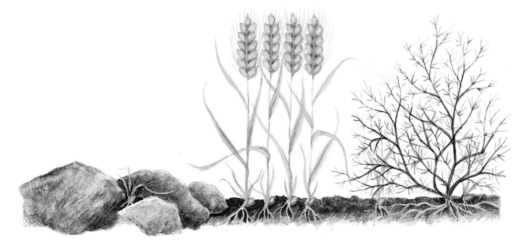

hear; but as they go on their way, they are choked by the cares and riches and pleasures of life, and their fruit does not mature. But as for that in the good soil, these are the ones who, when they hear the word, hold it fast in an honest and good heart, and bear fruit with patient endurance."

Parables of the Kingdom

He put before them another parable:
"The kingdom of heaven is like a mustard seed that someone took and sowed in his field; it is the smallest of all the seeds, but when it has grown it is the greatest of shrubs and becomes a tree, so that the birds of the air come and make nests in its branches."

"Again, the kingdom of heaven is like treasure hidden in a field, which someone found and hid; then in his joy he goes and sells all that he has and buys that field.

"Again, the kingdom of heaven is like a merchant in search of fine pearls; on finding one pearl of great value, he went and sold all that he had and bought it.

"Again, the kingdom of heaven is like a net that was thrown into the sea and caught fish of every kind; when it was full, they drew it ashore, sat down, and put the good into baskets but threw out the bad. So it will be at the end of the age. The angels will come out and separate the evil from the righteous and throw them into the furnace of fire, where there will be weeping and gnashing of teeth."

Jesus Stills the Storm

On that day, when evening had come, *Jesus* said to *the disciples*, "Let us go across to the other side." And leaving the crowd behind, they took him with them in the boat, just as he was. Other boats were with him.

A great windstorm arose, and the waves beat into the boat, so that the boat was already being swamped.

But he was in the stern, asleep on the cushion; and they woke him up and said to him, "Teacher, do you not care that we are perishing?"

He woke up and rebuked the wind, and said to the sea, "Peace! Be still!" Then the wind ceased, and there was a dead calm.

He said to them, "Why are you afraid? Have you still no faith?"

And they were filled with great awe and said to one another, "Who then is this, that even the wind and the sea obey him?"

The Daughter of Jairus

When Jesus had crossed again in the boat to the other side, a great crowd gathered around him; and he was by the sea. Then one of the leaders of the synagogue named Jairus came and, when he saw him, fell at his feet and begged him repeatedly, "My little daughter is at the point of death. Come and lay your hands on her, so that she may be made well, and live." So he went with him.

A large crowd followed him and pressed in on him. Now there was a woman who had been suffering from hemorrhages for twelve years. She had endured much under many physicians, and had spent all that she had; and she was no better, but rather grew worse.

She had heard about Jesus, and came up behind him in the crowd and touched his cloak, for she said, "If I but touch his clothes, I will be made well." Immediately her hemorrhage stopped; and she felt in her body that she was healed of her disease.

Immediately aware that power had gone forth from him, Jesus turned about in the crowd and said, "Who touched my clothes?" And his disciples said to him, "You see the crowd pressing in on you; how can you say, 'Who touched me?' " He looked all around to see who had done it.

But the woman, knowing what had happened to her, came in fear and trembling, fell down before him, and told him the whole truth. He said to her, "Daughter, your faith has made you well; go in peace, and be healed of your disease."

While he was still speaking, some people came from the leader's house to say, "Your daughter is dead. Why trouble the teacher any further?"

But overhearing what they said, Jesus said to the leader of the synagogue, "Do not fear, only believe." He allowed no one to follow him except Peter, James, and John, the brother of James.

When they came to the house of the leader of the synagogue, he saw a commotion, people weeping and wailing loudly. When he had entered, he said to them, "Why do you make a commotion and weep? The child is not dead but sleeping." And they laughed at him.

Then he put them all outside, and took the child's father and mother and those who were with him, and went in where the child was. He took her by the hand and said to her, "Talitha cum," which means, "Little girl, get up!" And immediately the girl got up and began to walk about (she was twelve years of age).

At this they were overcome with amazement. He strictly ordered them that no one should know this, and told them to give her something to eat. And the report of this spread throughout that district.

Jesus at Nazareth

He left that place and came to his hometown, and his disciples followed him.

On the sabbath he began to teach in the synagogue, and many who heard him were astounded. They said, "Where did this man get all this? What is this wisdom that has been given to him? What deeds of power are being done by his hands! Is not this the carpenter, the son of Mary and brother of James and Joses and Judas and Simon, and are not his sisters here with us?" And they took offense at him.

Then Jesus said to them, "Prophets are not without honor, except in their hometown, and among their own kin, and in their own house." And he could do no deed of power there, except that he laid his hands on a few sick people and cured them. And he was amazed at their unbelief.

Then he went about among the villages teaching.

John Has a Question

When John heard in prison what the Messiah was doing, he sent word by his disciples and said to him, "Are you the one who is to come, or are we to wait for another?" Jesus answered them, "Go and tell John what you hear and see: the blind receive their sight, the lame walk, the lepers are cleansed, the deaf hear, the dead are raised, and the poor have good news brought to them."

As they went away, Jesus began to speak to the crowds about John: "What did you go out into the wilderness to look at? A reed shaken by the wind? Someone dressed in soft robes? Look, those who wear soft robes are in royal palaces. What then did you go out to see? A prophet? Yes, I tell you, and more than a prophet. This is the one about whom it is written,

'See, I am sending my messenger ahead of you,
who will prepare your way before you.'

Truly I tell you, among those born of women no one has arisen greater than John the Baptist; yet the least in the kingdom of heaven is greater than he."

The Death of John

At that time Herod the ruler heard reports about Jesus; and he said to his servants, "This is John the Baptist; he has been raised from the dead, and for this reason these powers are at work in him." For Herod had arrested John, bound him, and put him in prison on account of Herodias, his brother Philip's wife, because John had been telling him, "It is not lawful for you to have her." Though Herod wanted to put him to death, he feared the crowd, because they regarded him as a prophet.

But when Herod's birthday came, the daughter of Herodias danced before the company, and she pleased Herod so much that he promised on oath to grant her whatever she might ask. Prompted by her mother, she said, "Give me the head of John the Baptist here on a platter."

The king was grieved, yet out of regard for his oaths, he sent and had John beheaded in the prison. The head was brought on a platter and given to the girl, who brought it to her mother. His disciples came and took the body and buried it; then they went and told Jesus.

The Twelve Are Sent Out

Jesus called the twelve and began to send them out two by two, and gave them authority over the unclean spirits. He ordered them to take nothing for their journey except a staff; no bread, no bag, no money in their belts; but to wear sandals and not to put on two tunics.

He said to them, "Wherever you enter a house, stay there until you leave the place. If any place will not welcome you and they refuse to hear you, as you leave, shake off the dust that is on your feet as a testimony against them."

So they went out and proclaimed that all should repent. They cast out many demons, and anointed with oil many who were sick and cured them.

Jesus Feeds Five Thousand

After this Jesus went to the other side of the Sea of Galilee, also called the Sea of Tiberias.

A large crowd kept following him, because they saw the signs that he was doing for the sick. Jesus went up the mountain and sat down there with his disciples. Now the Passover, the festival of the Jews, was near.

When he looked up and saw a large crowd coming toward him, he had compassion for them, because they were like sheep without a shepherd; and he began to teach them many things. *Then* Jesus said to Philip, "Where are we to buy bread for these people to eat?" He said this to test him, for he himself knew what he was going to do.

Philip answered him, "Six months' wages would not buy enough bread for each of them to get a little."

One of his disciples, Andrew, Simon Peter's brother, said to him, "There is a boy here who has five barley loaves and two fish. But what are they among so many people?"

Jesus said, "Make the people sit down." Now there was a great deal of grass in the place; so they sat down, about five thousand in all.

Then Jesus took the loaves, and when he had given thanks, he distributed them to those who were seated; so also the fish, as much as they wanted.

When they were satisfied, he told his disciples, "Gather up the fragments left over, so that nothing may be lost." So they gathered them up, and from the fragments of the five barley loaves, left by those who had eaten, they filled twelve baskets.

When the people saw the sign that he had done, they began to say, "This is indeed the prophet who is to come into the world." When Jesus realized that they were about to come and take him by force to make him king, he withdrew again to the mountain by himself.

Jesus and the Sabbath

One sabbath he was going through the grainfields; and as they made their way his disciples began to pluck heads of grain. The Pharisees said to him, "Look, why are they doing what is not lawful on the sabbath?" And he said to them, "Have you never read what David did when he and his companions were hungry and in need of food? He entered the house of God, when Abiathar was high priest, and ate the bread of the Presence, which it is not lawful for any but the priests to eat, and he gave some to his companions."

Then he said to them, "The sabbath was made for humankind, and not humankind for the sabbath; so the Son of Man is lord even of the sabbath."

214

The Good Samaritan

Then they sent to him some Pharisees and some Herodians to trap him in what he said. And they came and said to him, "Teacher, we know that you are sincere, and show deference to no one: for you do not regard people with partiality, but teach the way of God in accordance with truth. Is it lawful to pay taxes to the emperor, or not?"

But knowing their hypocrisy, he said to them, "Why are you putting me to the test? Bring me a denarius." And they brought one.

Then he said to them, "Whose head is this, and whose title?"

They answered, "The emperor's."

Jesus said to them, "Give to the emperor the things that are the emperor's, and to God the things that are God's." And they were utterly amazed at him.

Just then a lawyer stood up to test Jesus.

"Teacher," he said, "what must I do to inherit eternal life?"

He said to him, "What is written in the law? What do you read there?"

He answered, "You shall love the Lord your God with all your heart, and with all your soul, and with all your strength, and with all your mind; and your neighbor as yourself."

And he said to him, "You have given the right answer; do this, and you will live."

But wanting to justify himself, he asked Jesus, "And who is my neighbor?"

Jesus replied, "A man was going down from Jerusalem to Jericho, and fell into the hands of robbers, who stripped him, beat him, and went away, leaving him half dead. Now by chance a priest was going down that road; and when he saw him, he passed by on the other side. So likewise a Levite, when he came to the place and saw him, passed by on the other side.

"But a Samaritan while traveling came near him; and when he saw him, he was moved with pity. He went to him and bandaged his wounds, having poured oil and wine on them. Then he put him on his own animal, brought him to an inn, and took care of him. The next day he took out two denarii, gave them to the innkeeper, and said, 'Take care of him; and when I come back, I will repay you whatever more you spend.'

"Which of these three, do you think, was a neighbor to the man who fell into the hands of the robbers?" He said, "The one who showed him mercy." Jesus said to him, "Go and do likewise."

The Sermon on the Mount

When Jesus saw the crowds, he went up the mountain; and after he sat down, his disciples came to him. Then he began to speak, and taught them, saying:

"Blessed are the poor in spirit, for theirs is the kingdom of heaven.

"Blessed are those who mourn, for they will be comforted.

"Blessed are the meek, for they will inherit the earth.

"Blessed are those who hunger and thirst for righteousness, for they will be filled.

"Blessed are the merciful, for they will receive mercy.

"Blessed are the pure in heart, for they will see God.

"Blessed are the peacemakers, for they will be called children of God.

"Blessed are those who are persecuted for righteousness' sake, for theirs is the kingdom of heaven.

217

"Blessed are you when people revile you and persecute you and utter all kinds of evil against you falsely on my account. Rejoice and be glad, for your reward is great in heaven, for in the same way they persecuted the prophets who were before you.

"You have heard that it was said, 'An eye for an eye and a tooth for a tooth.' But I say to you, Do not resist an evildoer. But if anyone strikes you on the right cheek, turn the other also; and if anyone wants to sue you and take your coat, give your cloak as well; and if anyone forces you to go one mile, go also the

second mile. Give to everyone who begs from you, and do not refuse anyone who wants to borrow from you.

"You have heard that it was said, 'You shall love your neighbor and hate your enemy.' But I say to you, Love your enemies and pray for those who persecute you, so that you may be children of your Father in heaven; for he makes his sun rise on the evil and on the good, and sends rain on the righteous and on the unrighteous. For if you love those who love you, what reward

do you have? Do not even the tax collectors do the same? And if you greet only your brothers and sisters, what more are you doing than others? Do not even the Gentiles do the same? Be perfect, therefore, as your heavenly Father is perfect.

"Beware of practicing your piety before others in order to be seen by them; for then you have no reward from your Father in heaven.

"When you are praying, do not heap up empty phrases as the Gentiles do; for they think that they will be heard because of their many words. Do not be like them, for your Father knows what you need before you ask him. Pray then in this way:

Our Father in heaven,
  hallowed be your name,
  Your kingdom come,
  Your will be done,
    on earth as it is in heaven.
Give us this day our daily bread.
And forgive us our debts,
  as we also have forgiven our debtors.
And do not bring us to the time of trial,
  but rescue us from the evil one.

For if you forgive others their trespasses, your heavenly Father will also forgive you; but if you do not forgive others, neither will your Father forgive your trespasses.

"Do not store up for yourselves treasures on earth, where moth and rust consume and where thieves break in and steal; but store up for yourselves treasures in heaven, where neither moth nor rust consumes and where thieves
do not break in and steal.
For where your treasure is,
there your heart will be also.
No one can serve two
masters; for a slave will
either hate the one and love
the other, or be devoted
to the one and despise
the other. You cannot serve
God and wealth."

When Jesus had finished saying these things, the crowds were astounded at his teaching, for he taught them as one having authority, and not as their scribes.

Jesus Leaves Galilee

The Faith of a Foreigner

Jesus left that place and went away to the district of Tyre and Sidon. Just then a Canaanite woman from that region came out and started shouting, "Have mercy on me, Lord, Son of David; my daughter is tormented by a demon." But he did not answer her at all. And his disciples came and urged him, saying, "Send her away, for she keeps shouting after us." He answered, "I was sent only to the lost sheep of the house of Israel."

But she came and knelt before him, saying, "Lord, help me." He answered, "It is not fair to take the children's food and throw it to the dogs." She said, "Yes, Lord, yet even the dogs eat the crumbs that fall from their masters' table." Then Jesus answered her, "Woman, great is your faith! Let it be done for you as you wish." And her daughter was healed instantly.

Then he returned from the region of Tyre, and went by way of Sidon towards the Sea of Galilee, in the region of the Decapolis. They brought to him a deaf man who had an impediment in his speech; and they begged him to lay his hand on him. He took him aside in private, away from the crowd, and put his fingers into his ears, and he spat and touched his tongue. Then looking up to heaven, he sighed and said to him, "Ephphatha," that is, "Be opened." And immediately his ears were opened, his tongue was released, and he spoke plainly.

Then Jesus ordered them to tell no one; but the more he ordered them, the more zealously they proclaimed it.

They were astounded beyond measure, saying, "He has done everything well; he even makes the deaf to hear and the mute to speak."

The Persistent Pray-er

Jesus said to his disciples,
"Suppose one of you has a friend, and you go to him at midnight and say to him, 'Friend, lend me three loaves of bread; for a friend of mine has arrived, and I have nothing to set before him.' And he answers from within, 'Do not bother me; the door has already been locked, and my children are with me in bed; I cannot get up and give you anything.' I tell you, even though he will not get up and give him anything because he is his friend, at least because of his persistence he will get up and give him whatever he needs.

"So I say to you, Ask, and it will be given you; search, and you will find; knock, and the door will be opened for you. For everyone who asks receives, and everyone who searches finds, and for everyone who knocks, the door will be opened.

"Is there anyone among you who, if your child asks for a fish, will give a snake instead of a fish? Or if the child asks for an egg, will give a scorpion?

"If you then, who are evil, know how to give good gifts to your children, how much more will the heavenly Father give the Holy Spirit to those who ask him!"

"You Are the Messiah"

Now when Jesus came into the district of Caesarea Philippi, he asked his disciples, "Who do people say that the Son of Man is?" And they said, "Some say John the Baptist, but others Elijah, and still others Jeremiah or one of the prophets."

He said to them, "But who do you say that I am?"

Simon Peter answered, "You are the Messiah, the Son of the living God."

And Jesus answered him, "Blessed are you, Simon son of Jonah! For flesh and blood has not revealed this to you, but my Father in heaven.

"And I tell you, you are Peter, and on this rock I will build my church, and the gates of Hades will not prevail against it. I will give you the keys of the kingdom of heaven, and whatever you bind on earth will be bound in heaven, and whatever you loose on earth will be loosed in heaven."

Then he sternly ordered the disciples not to tell anyone that he was the Messiah.

Jesus Talks about His Death

From that time on, Jesus began to show his disciples that he must go to Jerusalem and undergo great suffering at the hands of the elders and chief priests and scribes, and be killed, and on the third day be raised. And Peter took him aside and began to rebuke him, saying, "God forbid it, Lord! This must never happen to you."

But he turned and said to Peter, "Get behind me, Satan! You are a stumbling block to me; for you are setting your mind not on divine things but on human things."

Then Jesus told his disciples, "If any want to become my followers, let them deny themselves and take up their cross and follow me. For those who want to save their life will lose it, and those who lose their life for my sake will find it."

Jesus and the Children

People were bringing little children to him in order that he might touch them; and the disciples spoke sternly to them. But when Jesus saw this, he was indignant and said to them, "Let the little children come to me; do not stop them; for it is to such as these that the kingdom of God belongs. It is not the will of your Father in heaven that one of these little ones should be lost.

"Truly I tell you, whoever does not receive the kingdom of God as a little child will never enter it." And he took them up in his arms, laid his hands on them, and blessed them.

Jesus and the Rich Man

As he was setting out on a journey, a man ran up and knelt before him, and asked him, "Good Teacher, what must I do to inherit eternal life?" Jesus said to him, "Why do you call me good? No one is good but God alone. You know the commandments: 'You shall not murder; You shall not commit adultery; You shall not steal; You shall not bear false witness; You shall not defraud; Honor your father and mother.'" He said to him, "Teacher, I have kept all these since my youth."

Jesus, looking at him, loved him and said, "You lack one thing; go, sell what you own, and give the money to the poor, and you will have treasure in heaven; then come, follow me." When he heard this, he was shocked and went away grieving, for he had many possessions.

Jesus looked around and said to his disciples, "How hard it will be for those who have wealth to enter the kingdom of God!" And the disciples were perplexed at these words. But Jesus said to them again, "Children, how hard it is to enter the kingdom of God! It is easier for a camel to go through the eye of a needle than for someone who is rich to enter the kingdom of God."

They were greatly astounded and said, "Then who can be saved?" Jesus said, "For mortals it is impossible, but for God all things are possible."

Then Peter said, "Look, we have left our homes and followed you." And he said to them, "Truly I tell you, there is no one who has left house or wife or brothers or parents or children, for the sake of the kingdom of God, who will not get back very much more in this age, and in the age to come eternal life."

The Rich Man and Lazarus

Jesus said to his disciples, "Do not worry about what you will eat or what you will drink, or what you will wear. Is not life more than food, and the body more than clothing? Look at the birds of the air; they neither sow nor reap nor gather into barns, and yet your heavenly Father feeds them. Are you not of more value than they? And why do you worry about clothing? Consider the lilies of the field, how they grow; they neither toil nor spin, yet I tell you, even Solomon in all his glory was not clothed like one of these. But if God so clothes the grass of the field, will he not much more clothe you—you of little faith? Therefore do not worry, saying, 'What will we eat?' or 'What will we drink?' or 'What will we wear?' Your heavenly Father knows that you need all these things. But strive first for the kingdom of God and his righteousness, and all these things will be given to you as well."

Again, Jesus said, "There was a rich man who was dressed in purple and fine linen and who feasted sumptuously every day. And at his gate lay a poor man named Lazarus, covered with sores, who longed to satisfy his hunger with what fell from the rich man's table; even the dogs would come and lick his sores. The poor man died and was carried away by the angels to be with Abraham. The rich man also died and was buried.

"In Hades he looked up and saw Abraham far away with Lazarus by his side. He called out, 'Father Abraham, have mercy on me, and send Lazarus to dip the tip of his finger in water and cool my tongue; for I am in agony in these flames.'

"But Abraham said, 'Child, remember that during your lifetime you received your good things, and Lazarus in like manner

228

evil things; but now he is comforted here, and you are in agony. Besides all this, between you and us a great chasm has been fixed, so that those who might want to pass from here to you cannot do so, and no one can cross from there to us.'

"He said, 'Then, father, I beg you to send him to my father's house—for I have five brothers—that he may warn them, so that they will not also come into this place of torment.' Abraham replied, 'They have Moses and the prophets; they should listen to them.' He said, 'No, father Abraham; but if someone goes to them from the dead, they will repent.'

"He said to him, 'If they do not listen to Moses and the prophets, neither will they be convinced even if someone rises from the dead.'"

The Blind Man at Jericho

As *Jesus* and his disciples and a large crowd were leaving Jericho, Bartimaeus son of Timaeus, a blind beggar, was sitting by the roadside. When he heard a crowd going by, he asked what was happening. They told him, "Jesus of Nazareth is passing by."

When he heard that it was Jesus, he began to shout out and

say, "Jesus, Son of David, have mercy on me!" Many sternly ordered him to be quiet, but he cried out even more loudly, "Son of David, have mercy on me!"

Jesus stood still and said, "Call him here."

And they called the blind man, saying to him, "Take heart; get up, he is calling you." So throwing off his cloak, he sprang up and came to Jesus.

Then Jesus said to him, "What do you want me to do for you?"

The blind man said to him, "My teacher, let me see again."

Jesus said to him, "Receive your sight; your faith has made you well."

Immediately he regained his sight and followed him, glorifying God; and all the people, when they saw it, praised God.

Zacchaeus

Jesus entered Jericho and was passing through it. A man was there named Zacchaeus; he was a chief tax collector and was rich. He was trying to see who Jesus was, but on account of the crowd he could not, because he was short in stature. So he ran ahead and climbed a sycamore tree to see him, because he was going to pass that way.

When Jesus came to the place, he looked up and said to him, "Zacchaeus, hurry and come down; for I must stay at your house today."

So he hurried down and was happy to welcome him.

All who saw it began to grumble and said, "He has gone to be the guest of one who is a sinner."

Zacchaeus stood there and said to the Lord, "Look, half of my possessions, Lord, I will give to the poor; and if I have defrauded anyone of anything, I will pay back four times as much."

Then Jesus said to him, "Today salvation has come to this

house, because he too is a son of Abraham. For the Son of Man came to seek out and to save the lost."

The Parable of the Money

Jesus told this parable:
"A nobleman went to a distant country to get royal power for himself and then return. He summoned ten of his slaves, and gave them ten pounds, and said to them, 'Do business with these until I come back.'

When he returned, he ordered these slaves to be summoned so that he might find out what they had gained by trading. The first came forward and said, 'Lord, your pound has made ten more pounds.' He said to him, 'Well done, good slave! Because you have been trustworthy in a very small thing, take charge of ten cities.'

Then the second came, saying, 'Lord, your pound has made five pounds.' He said to him, 'And you, rule over five cities.'

The the other came, saying, 'Lord, here is your pound. I wrapped it up in a piece of cloth, for I was afraid of you.' He said to him, 'Why then did you not put my money into the bank?' Then when I returned, I could have collected it with interest.'

He said, 'Take the pound from him and give it to the one who has ten pounds. I tell you, to all those who have, more will be given; but from those who have nothing, even what they have will be taken away.'"

The Father Who Waited

Jesus told this parable: "What woman having ten silver coins, if she loses one of them, does not light a lamp, sweep the house, and search carefully until she finds it? When she has found it, she calls together her friends and neighbors, saying 'Rejoice with me, for I have found the coin that I had lost.' Just so, I tell you, there is joy in the presence of the angels of God over one sinner who repents."

232

Then Jesus said, "There was a man who had two sons. The younger of them said to his father, 'Father, give me the share of the property that will belong to me.' So he divided his property between them.

"A few days later the younger son gathered all he had and traveled to a distant country, and there he squandered his property in dissolute living. When he had spent everything, a severe famine took place throughout that country, and he began to be in need. So he went and hired himself out to one of the citizens of that country, who sent him to his fields to feed the pigs. He would gladly have filled himself with the pods that the pigs were eating; and no one gave him anything.

"But when he came to himself he said, 'How many of my father's hired hands have bread enough and to spare, but here I am dying of hunger! I will get up and go to my father, and I will say to him, "Father, I have sinned against heaven and before you; I am no longer worthy to be called your son; treat me like one of your hired hands." '

"So he set off and went to his father. But while he was still far off, his father saw him and was filled with compassion; he ran and put his arms around him and kissed him. Then the son said to him, 'Father, I have sinned against heaven and before you; I am no longer worthy to be called your son.'

But the father said to his slaves, 'Quickly, bring out a robe—the best one—and put it on him; put a ring on his finger and sandals on his feet. And get the fatted calf and kill it, and let us eat and celebrate; for this son of mine was dead and is alive again; he was lost and is found!' And they began to celebrate.

"Now his elder son was in the field; and when he came and approached the house, he heard music and dancing. He called one of the slaves and asked what was going on. He replied, 'Your brother has come, and your father has killed the fatted calf, because he has got him back safe and sound.' Then he became angry and refused to go in.

"His father came out and began to plead with him. But he answered his father, 'Listen! For all these years I have been working like a slave for you, and I have never disobeyed your command; yet you have never given me even a young goat so that I might celebrate with my friends. But when this son of yours came back, who has devoured your property with prostitutes, you killed the fatted calf for him!'

"Then the father said to him, 'Son, you are always with me, and all that is mine is yours. But we had to celebrate and rejoice, because this brother of yours was dead and has come to life; he was lost and has been found.'"

Jesus in Jerusalem

The Triumphal Entry

When they were approaching Jerusalem, at Bethphage and Bethany, near the Mount of Olives, *Jesus* sent two of his disciples and said to them, "Go into the village ahead of you, and immediately as you enter it, you will find tied there a colt that has never been ridden; untie it and bring it. If anyone says to you, 'Why are you doing this?' just say this, 'The Lord needs it and will send it back here immediately.'"

This took place to fulfill what had been spoken through the prophet, saying,

> "Tell the daughter of Zion,
> Look, your king is coming to you,
> Humble, and mounted on a donkey,
>   and on a colt, the foal of a donkey."

They went away and found a colt tied near a door, outside in the street. As they were untying it, some of the bystanders said to them, "What are you doing, untying the colt?" They told them what Jesus had said; and they allowed them to take it.

Then they brought the colt to Jesus and threw their cloaks on it; and he sat on it. Many people spread their cloaks on the road, and others spread leafy branches that they had cut in the fields. Then those who went ahead and those who followed were shouting,

> "Hosanna!
>   Blessed is the one who comes in the name of the Lord!
>   Blessed is the coming kingdom of our ancestor David!
> Hosanna in the highest heaven!"

When he entered Jerusalem, the whole city was in turmoil, asking, "Who is this?" The crowds were saying, "This is the prophet Jesus from Nazareth in Galilee."

Some of the Pharisees in the crowd said to him, "Teacher, order your disciples to stop." He answered, "I tell you, if these were silent, the stones would shout out."

As he came near and saw the city, he wept over it, saying, 'If you, even you, had only recognized on this day the things that make for peace! But now they are hidden from your eyes. Indeed, the days will come upon you, when your enemies will set up ramparts around you and surround you, and hem you in on every side. They will not leave one stone upon another, because you did not recognize the time of your visitation from God." Then he entered Jerusalem and went into the temple; and when he had looked around at everything, as it was already late, he went out to Bethany with the twelve.

Mary and Martha

Now as they went on their way, he entered a certain village, where a woman named Martha welcomed him into her home. She had a sister named Mary, who sat at the Lord's feet and listened to what he was saying. But Martha was distracted by her many tasks; so she came to him and asked, "Lord, do you not care that my sister has left me to do all the work by myself? Tell her then to help me."

But the Lord answered her, "Martha, Martha, you are worried and distracted by many things; there is need of only one thing. Mary has chosen the better part, which will not be taken away from her."

Jesus Cleanses the Temple

Then they came again to Jerusalem. In the temple he found people selling cattle, sheep, and doves, and the money changers seated at their tables.

Making a whip of cords, he drove all of them out of the temple, both the sheep and the cattle. He also poured out the coins of the money changers and overturned their tables.

He told those who were selling the doves, "Take these things out of here! Stop making my Father's house a marketplace!" "Is it not written,

'My house shall be called a house of prayer for all the nations'?
But you have made it a den of robbers."

His disciples remembered that it was written, "Zeal for your house will consume me."

When the chief priests and the scribes heard it, they kept looking for a way to kill him; for they were afraid of him, because the whole crowd was spellbound by his teaching.

They said to Jesus, "By what authority are you doing these things? Who gave you this authority to do them?"

Jesus said to them, "I will ask you one question; answer me, and I will tell you by what authority I do these things. Did the baptism of John come from heaven, or was it of human origin? Answer me."

They argued with one another, "If we say, 'From heaven,' he will say, 'Why then did you not believe him?' But shall we say, 'Of human origin'?"—they were afraid of the crowd, for all regarded John as truly a prophet.

So they answered Jesus, "We do not know." And Jesus said to them, "Neither will I tell you by what authority I am doing these things."

When evening came, Jesus and his disciples went out of the city.

A Woman Anoints Jesus

While he was at Bethany in the house of Simon the leper, as he sat at the table, a woman came with an alabaster jar of very costly ointment of nard, and she broke open the jar and poured the ointment on his head. But some were there who said to one another in anger, "Why was the ointment wasted in this way? For this ointment could have been sold for more than three hundred denarii, and the money given to the poor." And they scolded her.

But Jesus said, "Let her alone; why do you trouble her? She has performed a good service for me. For you always have the poor with you, and you can show kindness to them whenever you wish; but you will not always have me. She has done what she could; she has anointed my body beforehand for its burial. Truly I tell you, wherever the good news is proclaimed in the whole world, what she has done will be told in remembrance of her."

Then Satan entered into Judas called Iscariot, who was one of the twelve; he went away and conferred with the chief priests and officers of the temple police about how he might betray him to them.

They were greatly pleased and agreed to give him money. So he consented and began to look for an opportunity to betray him to them when no crowd was present.

Preparing for the Passover

On the first day of Unleavened Bread, when the Passover lamb is sacrificed, his disciples said to him, "Where do you want us to go and make the preparations for you to eat the Passover?" So he sent two of his disciples, saying to them, "Go into the city, and a man carrying a jar of water will meet you; follow him, and wherever he enters, say to the owner of the house, 'The Teacher asks, Where is my guest room where I may eat the Passover with my disciples?' He will show you a large room upstairs, furnished and ready. Make preparations for us there." So the disciples set out and went to the city, and found everything as he had told them; and they prepared the Passover meal.

During supper Jesus got up from the table, took off his outer robe, and tied a towel around himself. Then he poured water into a basin and began to wash the disciples' feet and to wipe them with the towel that was tied around him.

He came to Simon Peter, who said to him, "Lord, are you going to wash my feet?"

Jesus answered, "You do not know now what I am doing, but later you will understand." Peter said to him, "You will never wash my feet."

Jesus answered, "Unless I wash you, you have no share with me." Simon Peter said to him, "Lord, not my feet only but also my hands and my head!"

Jesus said to him, "One who has bathed does not need to wash, except for the feet, but is entirely clean. And you are clean, though not all of you." For he knew who was to betray him; for this reason he said, "Not all of you are clean."

The Last Supper

While they were eating, Jesus said, "Truly I tell you, one of you will betray me." And they became greatly distressed and began to say to him one after another, "Surely not I, Lord?" He answered, "The one who has dipped his hand into the bowl with me will betray me. The Son of Man goes as it is written of him, but woe to that one by whom the Son of Man is betrayed! It would have been better for that one not to have been born." Judas, who betrayed him, said, "Surely not I, Rabbi?" He replied,

"You have said so."

While they were eating, Jesus took a loaf of bread, and after blessing it he broke it, gave it to the disciples, and said, "Take, eat; this is my body." Then he took a cup, and after giving thanks he gave it to them, saying, "Drink from it, all of you; for this is my blood of the covenant, which is poured out for many for the forgiveness of sins. I tell you, I will never again drink of this fruit of the vine until that day when I drink it new with you in my Father's kingdom."

When they had sung the hymn, they went out to the Mount of Olives.

Then Jesus said to them, "You will all become deserters because of me this night; for it is written,

'I will strike the shepherd,
and the sheep of the flock will be scattered.'

But after I am raised up, I will go ahead of you to Galilee." Peter said to him, "Though all become deserters because of you, I will never desert you." Jesus said to him, "Truly I tell you, this very night, before the cock crows, you will deny me three times." Peter said to him, "Even though I must die with you, I will not deny you." And so said all the disciples.

Gethsemane

Then Jesus went with them to a place called Gethsemane; and he said to his disciples, "Sit here while I go over there and pray." He took with him Peter and the two sons of Zebedee, and began to be grieved and agitated.

Then he said to them, "I am deeply grieved, even to death; remain here, and stay awake with me." And going a little farther, he threw himself on the ground and prayed, "My Father, if it is possible, let this cup pass from me; yet not what I want but what you want."

Then he came to the disciples and found them sleeping; and he said to Peter, "So, could you not stay awake with me one hour? Stay awake and pray that you may not come into the time of trial; the spirit indeed is willing, but the flesh is weak."

Again he went away for the second time and prayed, "My Father, if this cannot pass unless I drink it, your will be done." Again he came and found them sleeping, for their eyes were heavy. So leaving them again, he went away and prayed for the third time, saying the same words.

Then he came to the disciples and said to them, "Are you still sleeping and taking your rest? See, the hour is at hand, and the Son of Man is betrayed into the hands of sinners. Get up, let us be going. See, my betrayer is at hand."

Jesus Is Arrested

While he was still speaking, Judas, one of the twelve, arrived; with him was a large crowd with swords and clubs, from the chief priests and the elders of the people. Now the betrayer had given them a sign, saying, "The one I will kiss is the man; arrest him." At once he came up to Jesus and said, "Greetings, Rabbi!" and kissed him. Jesus said to him, "Friend, do what you are here to do." Then they came and laid hands on Jesus and arrested him. Suddenly, one of those with Jesus put his hand on his sword, drew it, and struck the slave of the high priest, cutting off his ear. Then Jesus said to him, "Put your sword back into its place; for all who take the sword will perish by the sword. Do you think that I cannot appeal to my Father, and he will at once send me more than twelve legions of angels? But how then would the scriptures be fulfilled, which say it must happen in this way?"

At that hour Jesus said to the crowds, "Have you come out with swords and clubs to arrest me as though I were a bandit? Day after day I sat in the temple teaching, and you did not arrest me. But all this has taken place, so that the scriptures of the prophets may be fulfilled." Then all the disciples deserted him and fled.

Jesus Appears before the Council

So the crowd that had arrived with Judas took Jesus to the high priest; and all the chief priests, the elders, and the scribes were assembled. Peter had followed him at a distance, right into the courtyard of the high priest; and he was sitting with the guards, warming himself at the fire.

Now the chief priests and the whole council were looking for testimony against Jesus to put him to death; but they found none. For many gave false testimony against him, and their testimony did not agree.

Some stood up and gave false testimony against him, saying, "We heard him say, 'I will destroy this temple that is made with hands, and in three days I will build another, not made with hands.'" But even on this point their testimony did not agree.

Then the high priest stood up before them and asked Jesus, "Have you no answer? What is it that they testify against you?" But he was silent and did not answer. Again the high priest asked him, "Are you the Messiah, the Son of the Blessed One?"

Jesus said, "I am; and

'you will see the Son of Man
seated at the right hand of the Power,'
and 'coming with the clouds of heaven.'"

Then the high priest tore his clothes and said, "Why do we still need witnesses? You have heard his blasphemy! What is your decision?" All of them condemned him as deserving death. Some began to spit on him, to blindfold him, and to strike him, saying to him, "Prophesy!" The guards also took him over and beat him.

Peter Denies Jesus

While Peter was below in the courtyard, one of the servant-girls of the high priest came by.

When she saw Peter warming himself, she stared at him and said, "You also were with Jesus, the man from Nazareth."

But he denied it, saying, "I do not know or understand what you are talking about." And he went out into the forecourt.

Then the cock crowed. And the servant-girl, on seeing him, began again to say to the bystanders, "This man is one of them." But again he denied it.

Then after a little while the bystanders again said to Peter, "Certainly you are one of them; for you are a Galilean."

But he began to curse, and he swore an oath, "I do not know this man you are talking about."

At that moment the cock crowed for the second time. Then Peter remembered that Jesus had said to him, "Before the cock crows twice, you will deny me three times." And he broke down and wept.

Jesus Appears before Pontius Pilate

As soon as it was morning, the chief priests held a consultation with the elders and scribes and the whole council. They bound Jesus, led him away, and handed him over to Pilate. Pilate asked him, "Are you the King of the Jews?" He answered him, "You say so."

Then the chief priests accused him of many things. Pilate asked him again, "Have you no answer? See how many charges they bring against you." But Jesus made no further reply, so that Pilate was amazed.

Now at the festival he used to release a prisoner for them, anyone for whom they asked. Now a man called Barabbas was in prison with the rebels who had committed murder during the insurrection. So the crowd came and began to ask Pilate to do for them according to his custom. Then he answered them, "Do you want me to release for you the King of the Jews?" For he realized that it was out of jealousy that the chief priests had handed him over.

But the chief priests stirred up the crowd to have him release Barabbas for them instead. Pilate spoke to them again, "Then what do you wish me to do with the man you call the King of the Jews?" They shouted back, "Crucify him!" Pilate asked them, "Why, what evil has he done?" But they shouted all the more, "Crucify him!"

So Pilate, wishing to satisfy the crowd, released Barabbas for them; and after flogging Jesus, he handed him over to be crucified.

The Crucifixion

Then the soldiers led him into the courtyard of the palace (that is, the governor's headquarters); and they called together the whole cohort. And they clothed him in a purple cloak; and after twisting some thorns into a crown, they put it on him. And they began saluting him, "Hail, King of the Jews!" They struck his head with a reed, spat upon him, and knelt down in homage to him.

After mocking him, they stripped him of the purple cloak and put his own clothes on him. Then they led him out to crucify him.

They compelled a passer-by, who was coming in from the country, to carry his cross; it was Simon of Cyrene, the father of Alexander and Rufus. Then they brought Jesus to the place called Golgotha (which means the place of a skull). And they offered him wine mixed with myrrh; but he did not take it. And they crucified him, and divided his clothes among them, casting lots to decide what each should take.

It was nine o'clock in the morning when they crucified him. The inscription of the charge against him read, "The King of the Jews." And with him they crucified two bandits, one on his right and one on his left.

Those who passed by derided him, shaking their heads and saying, "Aha! You who would destroy the temple and build it in three days, save yourself, and come down from the cross!" In the same way the chief priests, along with the scribes, were also mocking him among themselves and saying, "He saved others; he cannot save himself. Let the Messiah, the King of Israel, come down from the cross now, so that we may see and believe."

One of the criminals who were hanged there kept deriding him and saying, "Are you not the Messiah? Save yourself and us!" But the other rebuked him, saying, "Do you not fear God, since you are under the same sentence of condemnation. And we indeed have been condemned justly, for we are getting what we deserve for our deeds, but this man has done nothing wrong." Then he said, "Jesus, remember me when you come into your kingdom."

He replied, "Truly I tell you, today you will be with me in Paradise."

When it was noon, darkness came over the whole land until three in the afternoon. At three o'clock Jesus cried out with a loud voice, "Eloi, Eloi, lema sabachthani?" which means, "My God, my God, why have you forsaken me?"

When some of the bystanders heard it, they said, "Listen, he is calling for Elijah." And someone ran, filled a sponge with sour wine, put it on a stick, and gave it to him to drink, saying, "Wait, let us see whether Elijah will come to take him down."

Then Jesus gave a loud cry and breathed his last. And the curtain of the temple was torn in two, from top to bottom. Now

when the centurion, who stood facing him, saw that in this way he breathed his last, he said, "Truly this man was God's Son!"

There were also women looking on from a distance; among them were Mary Magdalene, and Mary the mother of James the younger and of Joses, and Salome. These used to follow him and provided for him when he was in Galilee; and there were many other women who had come up with him to Jerusalem.

The Burial

When evening had come, and since it was the day of Preparation, that is, the day before the sabbath, Joseph of Arimathea, a respected member of the council, who was also himself waiting expectantly for the kingdom of God, went boldly to Pilate and asked for the body of Jesus.

Then Pilate wondered if he were already dead; and summoning the centurion, he asked him whether he had been dead for some time. When he learned from the centurion that he was dead, he granted the body to Joseph. Then Joseph bought a linen cloth, and taking down the body, wrapped it in the linen cloth, and laid it in a tomb that had been hewn out of the rock. He then rolled a stone against the door of the tomb. Mary Magdalene and Mary the mother of Joses saw where the body was laid.

Jesus Is Raised

When the sabbath was over, Mary Magdalene, and Mary the mother of James, and Salome bought spices, so that they might go and anoint him. And very early on the first day of the week, when the sun had risen, they went to the tomb. They had been saying to one another, "Who will roll away the stone for us from the entrance to the tomb?" When they looked up, they saw that the stone, which was very large, had already been rolled back.

As they entered the tomb, they saw a young man, dressed in a white robe, sitting on the right side; and they were alarmed. But he said to them, "Do not be alarmed; you are looking for Jesus of Nazareth, who was crucified. He has been raised; he is not here. Look, there is the place they laid him. But go, tell his disciples and Peter that he is going ahead of you to Galilee; there you will see him, just as he told you." So they went out and fled from the tomb, for terror and amazement had seized them; and they said nothing to anyone, for they were afraid.

Now after he rose early on the first day of the week, he appeared first to Mary Magdalene, from whom he had cast out seven

demons. She went out and told those who had been with him, while they were mourning and weeping. But when they heard that he was alive and had been seen by her, they would not believe it.

The Meeting on the Way to Emmaus

Now on that same day two of them were going to a village called Emmaus, about seven miles from Jerusalem, and talking with each other about all these things that had happened. While they were talking and discussing, Jesus himself came near and went with them, but their eyes were kept from recognizing him. And he said to them, "What are you discussing with each other while you walk along?"

They stood still, looking sad. Then one of them, whose name was Cleopas, answered him, "Are you the only stranger in Jerusalem who does not know the things that have taken place there in these days?" He asked them, "What things?" They replied, "The things about Jesus of Nazareth, who was a prophet mighty in deed and word before God and all the people, and how our chief priests and leaders handed him over to be condemned to death and crucified him. But we had hoped that he was the one to redeem Israel. Yes, and besides all this, it is now the third day since these things took place. Moreover, some women of our group astounded us. They were at the tomb early this morning, and when they did not find his body there, they came back and told us that they had indeed seen a vision of angels who said that he was alive. Some of those who were with us went to the tomb and found it just as the women had said; but they did not see him."

Then he said to them, "Oh, how foolish you are, and how slow of heart to believe all that the prophets have declared! Was it not necessary that the Messiah should suffer these things and then enter into his glory?" Then beginning with Moses and all the prophets, he interpreted to them the things about himself in all the scriptures.

As they came near the village to which they were going, he walked ahead as if he were going on. But they urged him strongly, saying, "Stay with us, because the day is now nearly over." So he went in to stay with them. When he was at the table with them, he took bread, blessed and broke it, and gave it to them. Then their eyes were opened, and they recognized him; and he vanished from their sight. They said to each other, "Were not our hearts burning within us while he was talking to us on the road, while he was opening the scriptures to us?"

That same hour they got up and returned to Jerusalem; and they found the eleven and their companions gathered together. They were saying, "The Lord has risen indeed, and he has appeared to Simon!" Then they told what had happened on the road.

Jesus Is Taken Up to Heaven

Now the eleven disciples went to Galilee, to the mountain to which Jesus had directed them. And Jesus came and said to them, All authority in heaven and on earth has been given to me. Go therefore and make disciples of all nations, baptizing them in the name of the Father and of the Son and of the Holy Spirit, and teaching them to obey everything that I have commanded you. And remember, I am with you always, to the end of the age.

"But you will receive power when the Holy Spirit has come upon you; and you will be my witnesses in Jerusalem, in all Judea and Samaria, and to the ends of the earth." When he had said this, as they were watching, he was lifted up, and a cloud took him out of their sight. While he was going and they were gazing up toward heaven, suddenly two men in white robes stood by them. They said, "Men of Galilee, why do you stand looking up toward heaven? This Jesus, who has been taken up from you into heaven, will come in the same way as you saw him go into heaven."

The Early Church

God Sends the Holy Spirit

Then they returned to Jerusalem. When the day of Pentecost had come, they were all together in one place. And suddenly from heaven there came a sound like the rush of a violent wind, and it filled the entire house where they were sitting. Divided tongues, as of fire, appeared among them, and a tongue rested on each of them. All of them were filled with the Holy Spirit and began to speak in other languages, as the Spirit gave them ability.

Now there were devout Jews from every nation living in Jerusalem. At this sound the crowd gathered and was bewildered, because each one heard them speaking in the native language of each. Amazed, they asked, "How is it that we hear, each of us, in our own native language? Parthians, Medes, Elamites, and residents of Mesopotamia, Judea and Cappadocia, Pontus and Asia, Phygia and Pamphylia, Egypt and the parts of Libya belonging to Cyrene, and visitors from Rome, both Jews and proselytes, Cretans and Arabs—in our own languages we hear them speaking about God's deeds of power? What does this mean?" But others sneered and said, "They are filled with new wine."

But Peter, standing with the eleven, raised his voice and addressed them, "Men of Judea and all who live in Jerusalem, listen to what I say. Indeed, these are not drunk, as you suppose, for it is only nine o'clock in the morning. No, this is what was spoken through the prophet Joel:

'In the last days it will be, God declares,
that I will pour out my Spirit upon all flesh,
    and your sons and your daughters shall prophesy.
Then everyone who calls on the name of the Lord shall be
    saved.'

"Jesus of Nazareth, a man attested to you by God with deeds of power, wonders, and signs that God did through him among you, as you yourselves know—this man you crucified and killed by the hands of those outside the law. But God raised him up, having freed him from death, because it was impossible for him to be held in its power. Being therefore exalted at the right hand of God, and having received from the Father the promise of the Holy Spirit, he has poured out this that you both see and hear. Therefore let the entire house of Israel know with certainty that God has made him both Lord and Messiah, this Jesus whom you crucified."

Now when they heard this, they were cut to the heart and said to Peter and to the other apostles, "Brothers, what should we do?" Peter said to them, "Repent, and be baptized every one of you in the name of Jesus Christ so that your sins may be forgiven; and you will receive the gift of the Holy Spirit. For the promise is for you, for your children, and for all who are far away, everyone whom the Lord our God calls to him." So those who welcomed his message were baptized, and that day about three thousand persons were added. They devoted themselves to the apostles' teaching and fellowship, to the breaking of bread and the prayers.

The Ethiopian Court Official

Then an angel of the Lord said to Philip, "Get up and go toward the south to the road that goes down from Jerusalem to Gaza." (This is a wilderness road.) So he got up and went.

Now there was an Ethiopian eunuch, a court official of the Candace, queen of the Ethiopians, in charge of her entire treasury. He had come to Jerusalem to worship and was returning home; seated in his chariot, he was reading the prophet Isaiah.

Then the Spirit said to Philip, "Go over to this chariot and join it." So Philip ran up to it and heard him reading the prophet Isaiah. He asked, "Do you understand what you are reading?" He replied, "How can I, unless someone guides me?" And he

invited Philip to get in and sit beside him. Now the passage of
the scripture that he was reading was this:

"Like a sheep he was led to the slaughter,
    and like a lamb silent before its shearer,
    so he does not open his mouth.
In his humiliation justice was denied him.
    Who can describe his generation?
    For his life is taken away from the earth."

The eunuch asked Philip, "About whom, may I ask you, does
the prophet say this, about himself or about someone else?" Then
Philip began to speak, and starting with this scripture, he proclaimed to him the good news about Jesus.

As they were going along the road, they came to some water;
and the eunuch said, "Look, here is water! What is to prevent
me from being baptized?" He commanded the chariot to stop,
and both of them, Philip and the eunuch, went down into the
water, and Philip baptized him.

When they came up out of the water, the Spirit of the Lord
snatched Philip away; the eunuch saw him no more, and went
on his way rejoicing.

But Philip found himself at Azotus, and as he was passing
through the region, he proclaimed the good news to all the towns
until he came to Caesarea.

Saul

Many of the priests and religious leaders in Jerusalem were angry because the disciples were proclaiming that Jesus was alive and was the Messiah. So a severe persecution began against the church. A Pharisee named Saul was one of the leaders.

He went to the high priest and asked him for letters to the synagogues at Damascus, so that if he found any who belonged to the Way, men or women, he might bring them bound to Jerusalem. Now as he was approaching Damascus, suddenly a light from heaven flashed around him. He fell to the ground and heard a voice saying to him, "Saul, Saul, why do you persecute me?" He asked, "Who are you, Lord?" The reply came, "I am Jesus, whom you are persecuting. But get up and enter the city, and you will be told what you are to do." The men who were traveling with him stood speechless because they heard the voice but saw no one. Saul got up from the ground, and though his eyes were open, he could see nothing; so they led him by the hand and brought him into Damascus. For three days he was without sight, and neither ate nor drank.

Now there was a disciple in Damascus named Ananias. The Lord said to him in a vision, "Get up and go to the street called Straight, and at the house of Judas look for a man of Tarsus named Saul. At this moment he is praying, and he has seen in a vision a man named Ananias come in and lay his hands on him so that he might regain his sight." But Ananias answered, "Lord, I have heard from many about this man, how much evil he has done to your saints in Jerusalem; and here he has authority from the chief priests to bind all who invoke your name." But the Lord said to him, "Go, for he is an instrument whom I have chosen to bring my name before Gentiles and kings and before the people of Israel; I myself will show him how much he must suffer for the sake of my name."

So Ananias went and entered the house. He laid his hands on Saul and said, "Brother Saul, the Lord Jesus, who appeared to you on your way here, has sent me so that you may regain your sight and be filled with the Holy Spirit." And immediately something like scales fell from his eyes, and his sight was restored. Then he got up and was baptized, and after taking some food, he regained his strength.

For several days he was with the disciples in Damascus, and immediately he began to proclaim Jesus in the synagogues, saying, "He is the Son of God." All who heard him were amazed and said, "Is not this the man who made havoc in Jerusalem among those who invoked this name? And has he not come here for the purpose of bringing them bound before the chief priests?" Saul became increasingly more powerful and confounded the Jews who lived in Damascus by proving that Jesus was the Messiah.

After some time had passed, the Jews plotted to kill him, but their plot became known to Saul. They were watching the gates day and night so that they might kill him; but his disciples took him by night and let him down through an opening in the wall, lowering him in a basket.

When he had come to Jerusalem, he attempted to join the disciples; and they were all afraid of him, for they did not believe that he was a disciple. But Barnabas took him, brought him to

260

the apostles, and described for them how on the road he had seen the Lord, who had spoken to him, and how in Damascus he had spoken boldly in the name of Jesus. So he went in and out among them in Jerusalem, speaking boldly in the name of the Lord.

Meanwhile the church throughout Judea, Galilee, and Samaria had peace and was built up. Living in the fear of the Lord and in the comfort of the Holy Spirit, it increased in numbers.

Lydia

Saul (now known as Paul) began to travel about the region, proclaiming the good news of salvation through Jesus wherever he went. Often Paul chose men to go with him on his travels. The following stories about Paul were written by one of his traveling companions.

One night Paul had a vision: there stood a man of Macedonia pleading with him and saying, "Come over to Macedonia and help us." When he had seen the vision, we immediately tried to cross over to Macedonia, being convinced that God had called us to proclaim the good news to them.

We remained in the city of Philippi for some days. On the sabbath day we went outside the gate by the river, where we supposed there was a place of prayer; and we sat down and spoke to the women who had gathered there. A certain woman named Lydia, a worshiper of God, was listening to us; she was from the city of Thyatira and a dealer in purple cloth. The Lord opened her heart to listen eagerly to what was said by Paul. When she and her household were baptized, she urged us, saying, "If you have judged me to be faithful to the Lord, come and stay at my home."

And she prevailed upon us.

Paul Is Imprisoned

One day, as we were going to the place of prayer, we met a slave-girl who had a spirit of divination and brought her owners a great deal of money by fortune-telling. While she followed Paul and us, she would cry out, "These men are slaves of the Most High God, who proclaim to you a way of salvation." She kept doing this for many days. But Paul, very much annoyed, turned and said to the spirit, "I order you in the name of Jesus Christ to come out of her." And it came out that very hour.

But when her owners saw that their hope of making money was gone, they seized Paul and Silas and dragged them before the authorities. They said, "These men are disturbing our city; they are Jews and are advocating customs that are not lawful for us as Romans to adopt or observe." The crowd joined in attacking them, and the magistrates had them stripped of their clothing and ordered them to be beaten with rods. After they had given them a severe flogging, they threw them into prison and ordered the jailer to keep them securely.

About midnight Paul and Silas were praying and singing hymns to God, and the prisoners were listening to them. Suddenly there was an earthquake, so violent that the foundations of the prison were shaken; and immediately all the doors were opened and everyone's chains were unfastened. When the jailer woke up and saw the prison doors wide open, he drew his sword and was about to kill himself, since he supposed that the prisoners had escaped. But Paul shouted in a loud voice, "Do not harm yourself, for we are all here."

The jailer called for lights, and rushing in, he fell down trembling before Paul and Silas. Then he brought them outside and said, "Sirs, what must I do to be saved?" They answered, "Believe on the Lord Jesus, and you will be saved, you and your household." They spoke the word of the Lord to him and to all who were in his house. At the same hour of the night he took them and washed their wounds; then he and his entire family were baptized without delay. He brought them up into the house and set food before them.

When morning came, the magistrates sent the police, saying, "Let those men go." And the jailer reported the message to Paul, saying, "The magistrates sent word to let you go; therefore come out now and go in peace." But Paul replied, "They have beaten us in public, uncondemned, men who are Roman citizens, and have thrown us into prison; and now are they going to discharge us in secret? Certainly not! Let them come and take us out themselves." The police reported these words to the magistrates, and they were afraid when they heard that they were Roman citizens; so they came and apologized to them.

Paul in Rome

Later, Paul was again put in prison. When two years had passed and his case had not been settled, he appealed to be tried before the emperor. He was then put on a ship sailing to Rome, the capital.

But soon a violent wind *arose*. We were being pounded by the storm so violently that on the next day they began to throw the cargo overboard, and on the third day with their own hands they threw the ship's tackle overboard. All hope of our being saved was at last abandoned.

In the morning they noticed a bay with a beach, on which they planned to run the ship ashore. But striking a reef, they ran the ship aground; the stern was being broken up by the force of the waves. The centurion ordered those who could swim to jump overboard first and make for the land, and the rest to follow on planks. And so it was that all were brought safely to land.

Three months later we set sail on a ship that had wintered at the island, and so we came to Rome. The believers from there, when they heard of us, came to meet us. On seeing them, Paul thanked God and took courage. When we came into Rome, Paul was allowed to live by himself, with the soldier who was guarding him.

He called together the local leaders of the Jews. He explained the gospel to them, testifying to the kingdom of God and trying to convince them about Jesus both from the law of Moses and from the prophets. Some were convinced by what he had said, while others refused to believe.

He lived there two whole years at his own expense and welcomed all who came to him, proclaiming the kingdom of God and teaching about the Lord Jesus Christ with all boldness and without hindrance.

List of Stories and Biblical References

270

About the Illustrator

Annegert Fuchshuber has been writing and illustrating children's books in her native Germany since 1968. A contributor to more than forty-five books, she has received numerous awards, including a 1990 Parents' Choice Award for her book *Giant Story—Mouse Tale* and fourteen European book awards. Also available in English are her books *The Cuckoo-Clock Cuckoo* and *From Dinosaurs to Fossils*. She lives in Augsburg, Germany. As part of her research and preparation for illustrating this story Bible, she made several trips to the Middle East.